Institutionalized and Happy

By: Bert Arnold

"Institutionalized and Happy," by Bert Arnold ISBN 978-1-63868-001-7 (softcover).

Published 2021 by Virtualbookworm.com Publishing Company Inc., P.O. Box 9949, College Station, TX 77842. Copyright 2021 by Bert Arnold. All rights reserved. No part of this publication may be reproduced, stored in a retrieval system, or transmitted in any form or by any means, electronic, mechanical, recording or otherwise, without the prior permission of Bert Arnold.

ACKNOWLEDGEMENTS

IT IS WITH GREAT LOVE AND GRATITUDE that I acknowledge all the time my neuroscientist grandson, Dr. Eric Arnold put into editing this book but also the patience and time he took to teach me some computer skills which expedited my writing. While he was editing for me he was also editing two doctoral papers, planning his termination in the lab at Duke to move to California, and keeping up with his running track. I will be forever grateful to you Eric.

I want to thank Kelley, his girlfriend, for loaning Eric to me on her time.

Our son, Dirk, and his wife who helped me with the computer as well. Dirk kept our condo in good repair and shopped for me so I could devote more time to writing. Thank you.

Patricia Shisler, our daughter, was willing to edit but I turned her down so she could be surprised by her uncle's stories. Thank you for understanding , Patricia.

How could I not thank LeRoy who persevered with me when I bugged him for details or for his willingness for me to write his memoirs.

Carol Riddle was a wonderful source for examining with me the deprivation issues we both felt as a result of our abandonments and placements at Bethany. Thank you Carol.

Bert Arnold

I thank my husband for tolerating late meals and lack of attention while I wrote. He has for 66 years been supportive of whatever I have attempted to do. No wonder I love him.

I thank Bobby Bernshausen at Virtualbookworm for publishing two books for me.

FROM THE AUTHOR

FIVE YEARS AGO I WROTE MY MEMOIRS in a book, "Somewhere Out There." I wrote it to explain how my life developed as a result of being institutionalized at Bethany Orphan's Home for fifteen years. The more I thought about my brother LeRoy, I realized that our means of survival and coping with the outside world were remarkably different. There are many ways of coping and our strategies went in two distinct directions.

I learned so much about my brother in writing this book. I thought I knew him inside and out. What a shock to know I had so much more to learn. My reasons for writing are threefold. First, I wanted to describe how years of institutionalization effect a person's life. I never guessed how much influence this had on LeRoy or on myself. Secondly, LeRoy wanted me to write for his children. He believes they will also learn a lot about him, as he often kept his daily activities to himself. Thirdly, it was wonderful to have a big project to do while quarantining during the COVID-19 pandemic. It certainly kept me from being bored!

You will find out that our family of Gensemer children were raised in an orphanage, Bethany Orphan's Home, and my intent is to share some of LeRoy's experiences there and how they affected his life. We coped in different ways but unlike me, LeRoy was a happy camper all his life.

Institutions per say are not bad. Well-staffed, caring institutions can be the best option for children who have been taken away from their family of origin and severely traumatized with feelings of abandonment. These children need a place that requires no bonding unless they bond by choice. Foster care and adoption, on the other hand, require bonding to be successful. Some of us are not looking for that type of relationship. We have been hurt too badly. The emotional pain a child feels when they are abandoned is too painful to face in its totality. Everyone needs the assurance that someone is there for them, even if that 'someone' is inadequate. There is no guarantee when professionals find a foster home or facilitate an adoption that it will be a successful placement. It is the luck of the draw. At Bethany, I chose to bond with a male staff member and a female staff member. LeRoy never found anyone he wanted to bond with. He chose to simply do what was expected of him and, as a result, he developed his own coping skills which served him quite well.

Bethany was a safe and comfortable home and haven for us. We will never be able to prove Bethany was the best placement for me and LeRoy but we believe it was. We believe our scars are from our home of origin and parental abandonment rather than from Bethany. Like any family it was far from perfect, but it was more than adequate for us. Many alumni feel it was home for them also, and bonded with the institution. Many returned for years and contributed their time and money to Bethany out of gratitude for what Bethany had done for them. LeRoy is one of those alumni who feels Bethany gave him the tools to become a contributing member of society and the ability to be happy all his life. I want to write about how LeRoy's life evolved and the effects his childhood had on him as an adult.

This book has been written with all the love in my heart for LeRoy. I took copious notes from each of our many interviews and tried to be as close to LeRoy's words and descriptions as I could. He provided me with many happy hours of his storytelling. Thank you for that, LeRoy.

Institutionalized and Happy

Our lives took different courses. He lived in Reading, Pennsylvania and I lived in Philadelphia, but we were in touch all these years. All through our 90+ years our love has never faltered. We remained best friends through thick and thin. I wonder if maybe in our home of origin he looked out for me. What a guy, my brother, LeRoy. Meet him.

CHAPTER 1:
BETHANY

When LeRoy and I grew up at Bethany, it was called Bethany Orphan's Home.

OUR MOTHER WAS OVERWHELMED with just a few children and by 1934 she had seven, which was much more than she could handle. She was unable to deal with her emotional problems while mothering, so she gave up on mothering rather than facing her situation. I went to visit her when I was an adult, feeling I could find out about my childhood as well as hers. Unfortunately, she was unable to remember those days and the visits were largely ungratifying. On our last visit, she said to me, "See that television over there? I used to love to watch it but not anymore." When I asked her why, her response was, "I think of what I did with my life and what I could have done." I felt she no longer needed to see me. I felt she was glad to see me but also pained, so there was nothing to be gained by torturing her further.

LeRoy's earliest memory in our house is of sleeping near our mother's silk petticoat which hung on a hanger near his bed and rubbing his hands on it until he fell asleep. This memory seems so vivid and essential for him to remember. It's like she gave him something of herself. He was comforted by it. He has no memory of interacting with his mother. She was just there. Think of how hungry that little boy must have been for nurturing.

Our older brother Sam (7) and LeRoy (5), spent their days on the street. They stayed outside all day looking at an icehouse, a grocery store, or a poor house. They were unaware of what people were doing in those places or what they were missing. Our mother was so overwhelmed that she must have sanctioned them to be out all day. Years later when LeRoy and I visited the old neighborhood, a woman who knew our family told us that all she remembers about our family is that the two oldest boys were always on the street. We assumed that because they were not troublemakers no one in the neighborhood complained about them. Those must have been the happiest hours of the boys lives up to that point. It is a shame these boys did not grow up as best friends but jealousy on the part of the oldest brother's wife kept them apart. Our father was unemployed most of the time which meant he was around the house too often. Many family meals were composed of turnips and potatoes three times a day. Our father grew them in our small backyard. Our sister hated turnips and remembered being punished every time she refused to eat them, which was often. We have no idea what our father did when he worked, but he did collect some unemployment according to our records, so at times he must have been gainfully employed.

Institutionalized and Happy

LeRoy vividly remembers the day our mother brought home the baby of our family. She walked three miles from the hospital in Shillington to our house. Terrible. LeRoy and Sam were in the backyard when she arrived carrying the baby. Our father told them to go into the room with the sink and he then proceeded to fight with her, throwing a chair at her. She came into the room with the sink, where the boys were standing, to wipe the blood from herself and the baby. When our father saw them witnessing this horror, he ordered them upstairs. Could that have been just a wee bit of trying to protect the boys? That might have been the most the boys got from him. No wonder LeRoy shut down emotionally at an early age.

Our father was the disciplinarian. LeRoy disliked him. He remembers being punished by him always in the same manner. He made LeRoy sit on the cellar steps with no light and told him that a "bogeyman" lived in the basement and rats were running free. LeRoy would sit there sobbing but there was never any concern shown by either parent. Our mother was probably already unable to think and grossly overwhelmed.

Our mother took a bus one day with LeRoy and baby Carl. LeRoy has no idea where they were headed but he remembers that once they sat down, she opened her blouse and took out a breast to feed Carl. LeRoy had no idea what was happening but took for granted it was normal because other women on the bus were doing the same thing. I asked how he felt about it and he said he felt nothing but thought it looked strange.

On September 27 in 1933, while LeRoy was 5, our father took himself up to the county prison and fatally shot himself on the grounds. He picked those grounds because his father was in jail for embezzlement of county funds when he worked in the courthouse. He left his father a note to apologize for what he had just done. He left no note for his children or wife. In our later years that would have helped us to feel he did have some feelings for us. Bethany records say Children's Aid Society thought he did it because he was depressed that he could not provide for us. Our mother failed to tell any of the children about his suicide but Sam and LeRoy accompanied her to the funeral. LeRoy peered into the coffin and remembers that he knew that meant he was dead. He felt nothing because he had been treated so badly. It was an unemotional experience for him.

In December of that same year the Children's Aid Society made three visits to our house (at the request of our father originally). We got this bit of information in 2020 when we were allowed a copy of our records at Bethany. Sometimes survival depends on those little signs of caring. According to our records they assume he shot himself out of desperation about his inability to care for us. Maybe I am grasping at straws, but if you grow up with no one loving you, it feels good to think maybe he did care and maybe even loved us.

They deemed our mother to be an "unfit mother" as they were called at that time and recommended taking all of us out of the house permanently. Our mother was further punished for being "unfit" and was told she could not visit us for five years. In the '30s there was no Department of Human Services or any agency to handle placements, so if children were to be placed outside of their homes, it generally occurred through the church. Our minister was sent to our house to evaluate whether it was appropriate for us to be raised at Bethany. He deemed us to be and we were recommended to be placed at Bethany Orphan's Home in Womelsdorf, Pennsylvania. LeRoy had no idea why either of these people were coming to visit but he was aware that they were occurring. He ascribed no significance to them. Bethany was an Evangelical and Reformed Church institution (called the United Church of Christ today). The church near our house was also of that denomination. Bethany took only children who were members of that denomination. I cringe when I think of what might have happened to us if Bethany had refused us.

Institutionalized and Happy

Bethany decided to take the six Gensemer children but not the oldest boy, Ted, because he was "illegitimate," as children born out of wedlock were called back then. At that time, to become a mother without the benefit of marriage was almost a crime and often the child was punished as well. We never did find out who raised him but later our mother told us that he had been taken away from her also. When LeRoy was an adult and working, a man came into his place of work and shook his hand and asked him if he knew LeRoy Gensemer. LeRoy told him he was LeRoy. The man said, "I am Ted Trivel. Your half-brother. Why don't you come visit me at my apartment?" which LeRoy did. Ted sat and read comic books until LeRoy got bored and told Ted he had to leave for a meeting and never saw him again. When our mother died, he called LeRoy and asked if he had inherited a $500 insurance policy our mother had taken out years before which made LeRoy the beneficiary. Ted said it should have been his and if LeRoy failed to turn it over to him, he would take him to court. LeRoy mailed it to him to avoid any problem. None of his other half brothers or sisters ever met him. He was a no-show at his mother's funeral but the Gensemer children were all in attendance.

Rev. Rhodes drove us to Bethany and, literally, dropped us off at the main building that housed the offices of Bethany. LeRoy remembers someone taking a picture of all of us on the lawn in front of the offices before sending all of us to the infirmary for a three day stay to check us for head lice or any other communicable diseases in order to protect the rest of the community. We were kept together in a playroom during the day, but how strange it must have been for us when nighttime came and we each had our own bed. The girls slept on one side and the boys on the other with a hall separating us and no visitation allowed. LeRoy remembers nothing of those three days.

CHAPTER 2:
FRICK COTTAGE

AFTER THEY DEEMED US HEALTHY, we were separated by cottages. My sister and I went to two different cottages but my two younger siblings went with me to the baby cottage. Baby Carl was in a separate room because he had "consumption" which was what tuberculosis was called back then. I could only see him through glass doors. LeRoy and Sam were sent to two different cottages also. As we were to learn, placement was calculated by age. For the rest of our time at Bethany we saw each other only at religious ceremonies such as Sunday school, church, and our nightly chapel services. The middle of the campus had playgrounds and sport areas so we couldn't see into each other's buildings. It was as if there was a line down the middle of the campus with boys on one side and girls on the other. After I turned six, none of us were together again except at religious services like nightly chapel. Eventually, we stopped looking for each other.

LeRoy was escorted to Frick cottage by a staff member. This cottage was for boys aged 5 to 7. Three adults supervised 25 boys. The couple who took responsibility for 25 boys oriented him to his bed and the kitchen then told him what his chores were going to be. There was one more person there as a support person for the couple. Then he had dinner. He was a stranger in a strange place and what made him happy was the other kids. He was accepted in a benign manner - that is, they accepted him without any fuss. His early traumas had numbed him so he was happy which he has been for the rest of his life.

Each morning when he woke up, he made his bed and got dressed. The boys then lined up outside of the dining room and repeated this poem:

> Heels together
> Hands behind your back
> And stand up straight
> And no talking at the table.

Then they marched into the dining room where they stood behind their chairs looking at their family-style breakfast, but they were unable to sit down to eat just yet. They all had Bible verses they had memorized before they could eat. LeRoy's verse was, "Let the words of my mouth and the meditation of my heart be acceptable in thy sight oh Lord, my strength and my redeemer." Fortunately, he said the same verse daily. This must have been a mouthwatering experience and frustrating as well to see food you were not allowed to eat until the rituals were performed. LeRoy and the boys would then sit down and eat in silence with a matron patrolling to make sure they remained silent. They had to eat quickly so they could go do their chores, and prepare themselves for school.

The reason we all worked so hard was because these were the Depression years. Every child on the campus had jobs except for those in the baby cottage. There were 257 children at that time. The highest number they ever had. It was imperative we all pitched in.

LeRoy's chores were to dry the dishes, set the table, clean the playroom, and to do some cleaning in other parts of the building. These were the jobs of the youngest of the 25 boys. The jobs were rotated so you could learn the skills required to take care of a home. LeRoy did what was required with a good attitude about work. Emotionally, he continued to clothe himself in a coat of armor to shut off his emotions and to free himself from any psychological pain, hurt, or anger. It was his method to remain happy and survive. He has always been happy by having goals, accomplishing those goals, and receiving satisfaction from a job well done, just as Bethany taught him to do. Behaving this way also kept the staff out of his hair.

As he became older, his chores changed. His chores passed on to the younger boys and his duties were to teach the younger children to memorize the alphabet and some elementary mathematics. He enjoyed this assignment.

Birthdays were not celebrated or mentioned so we were not aware of them. Apparently, the office knew our dates because we were told to move from cottage to cottage in the appropriate timeframe. Moving was based on age in every cottage. We have no idea how we found out our birthdays.

Frick cottage was next to Leinbach cottage where our sister Pearl lived. LeRoy looked out of the window one day at the swings and saw Pearl sitting on one of them sobbing hard. He could have gone to see her and comfort her but chose not to do so. He has no memory of why he chose not to go. Maybe his own pain made hers too much to deal with.

It was time for him to move on. Sometimes he moved alone and sometimes similarly-aged boys moved with him. He was told to pack up his clothes and move to Knerr cottage. By now he knew the campus so well that he could walk himself to the designated building. The toys he played with always stayed in the previous building. They were never ours.

CHAPTER 3: KNERR COTTAGE

ONE OF LEROY'S FIRST JOBS was to work in the boiler room located within the cottage. He wet pieces of asbestos and wrapped them around hot pipes to be sure everyone was protected from the hot pipes. Imagine a little boy doing such dangerous work! Bethany had no road in the middle of the campus, but one was surely needed for transporting items across the campus so one boy would take the ashes from the boiler and put them in a wheelbarrow to take to a designated spot. There LeRoy dumped them and raked them to get the road started. This too was dangerous, and LeRoy still bears a scar from spilling the hot ashes out of the wheelbarrow. When he burned himself, one of the boys bandaged it up and he never reported it to staff nor did he receive professional treatment which would have been available in the infirmary. The nurse was there 24/7. A road was finally put in and we simply called it "the dirt road" as that was what it looked like. As usual LeRoy had never told me this before and it pains me to think of the hardships he endured. No wonder he began to think and rebel when no one was around. He was 9 years old doing a man's work.

Food was an organized production and the same system for all cottages. Two children would go to the back of the main kitchen and pick up the meal. They were enclosed in large metal containers which fit into a metal holder and was carried to each cottage. The two children would carry it to each of their cottages. You ate whatever food was in the containers or you went hungry.

After the containers were clean, they were returned to the kitchen to be filled for the next meal. They could be so heavy we would have to take breaks on the way to our cottages.

On weekends the workload was lighter so the boys played lots of quoits and softball. LeRoy usually won and it was so nice to be able to be outside with no pressure from school or staff. He was always gracious about losing but he competed hard and won most of the time. He happily congratulated anyone who beat him. Of course, church and Sunday school came first.

Himmelreich's Grove was situated about half a mile from Bethany. It was in a beautiful setting cut out from the base of the mountains. Between Bethany and the grove was nothing but woods. What a beautiful place to grow up because there was beautiful flora and fauna everywhere around us. Even then I appreciated those things and would get relief walking the woods in the quiet of my own company.

The grove was built to accommodate hundreds of people who would pay to hear the country music (we called it hillbilly music) of Uncle Jack and Mary Lou, entertainers from Reading who sang and played guitars. The song we most remember is called "Dust on the Bible" which goes like this:

> *I went into a home one day just to see some friends of mine,*
> *Of all their books and magazines, not a Bible could I find.*
> *I asked them for the Bible when they brought it, what a shame,*
> *For the dust was covered o'er it, not a fingerprint was plain.*
> *Dust on the Bible, dust on the Holy Word,*
> *The words of all the prophets and the sayings of our Lord.*
> *Of all the other books you'll find, there's none salvation holds,*
> *Get the dust off the Bible and redeem your poor soul.*
> *Oh. You can read your magazines of love and tragic things,*
> *But not one word of Bible verse, not a scripture do you know.*
> *When it is the very truth and its contents good for you,*
> *But its dust is covered o'er it,*
> *And it's sure to doom your poor soul.*

This was one of the favorites of the crowd and would be requested over and over again.

Where LeRoy placed the snacks he stock from Himmelreich's Grove.

We Bethany kids knew how to sneak in over a fence that delineated the grove from the woods. We got in for free! The owners of the grove and Bethany must have known what we were doing because we seemed to be caught any place we sneaked except at the grove and we continually visited there, although Bethany called it off-limits. We suspect both Bethany and the grove people tolerated it because we were so well-behaved. Some of us were there every week and we were never caught unless we missed a meal or bedtime and we never caused trouble for anyone at the grove. We were just there. There goes that phrase again but it is so true. The music was mostly gospel but it was enticing and thrilling just to be there with a rare chance to see people who were not orphans and a thrill just to see the entertainers. Big time entertainers came on some Sundays such as Dale Evans and Gene Autry or the Ink Spots. At times, it got so crowded that people paid to stand in the back of the seating area in the woods. LeRoy was not interested in the entertainment. What he wanted was Uncle Jack and Mary Lou's snacks. Under the stage they kept a locked container with potato chips and other snacks which we never got at Bethany. He would go under the stage and use a bobby pin or a nail and open their locked box of goodies. He was never caught which makes me think they did not really mind his shenanigans. Seems like a possibility. Later you will find that LeRoy also had other things in mind when he visited the grove.

Nick Stick was a game he liked a lot. The guys carved a stick until it was pointed at both ends. Then on the four sides of the stick they wrote 1, 2, 3, or 4. That was the Nick. They laid that on cement and got another stick that was not carved and threw it at the Nick's pointed end. That made the Nick fly and whatever number it landed on, was your score. The person who reached 21 first was the winner. LeRoy won most of the time and he never cheated. When he won, he won fairly. The work ethic was so pounded into us that we had to do something different in our free time.

We had the most wonderful water at Bethany, which emanated from our reservoir in the mountains. The water was the clearest, most pure, and icy cold water I have ever had. How I long for that type of water again. LeRoy would go into the trash to find an empty quart bottle, wash it, fill it with hot water, and add to it some wild mint leaves. When he was satisfied it was brewed, he would retrieve it and have a delectable original delicious drink. What a treat and how luxurious it felt to him. Everyone on our campus loved to get down on their stomach and take their hand to the water and lap it up. It was so cold, satisfying and delicious.

During the Depression years if you filled your car or any vehicle with gasoline, the station would give you a free blue Depression glass with a picture of Shirley Temple on the bottom. She was a big Hollywood star and a little girl the whole country loved. Bethany apparently amassed quite a collection and LeRoy and some of the other boys had to dig a deep ditch and bury them.

Institutionalized and Happy

What an odd thing to do with glass. I wonder what they would be worth today. LeRoy knows where the spot is and often wonders with his ingenuity and all his trips back to Bethany why he never tried to unearth them.

Saturday night was a night the whole campus looked forward to because at Knerr, there was a movie shown in the auditorium. All except the baby cottage attended but again the boys sat on one side of an aisle and the girls on the other. To our knowledge no one ever broke that rule. LeRoy's all-time favorite was "Felix the Cat." We both remember the fear we felt in a series we loved titled "Chandu." They were very scary because people just sank to the bottom of quicksand and it looked so real to us.

I could not believe LeRoy when he told me this but unfortunately it is true, even if bizarre. I found it hard to write and to digest such a crazy story. It is a story LeRoy never shared with anyone before. When we talked about it, I asked him how he felt about it and I got his usual answer, "I never thought anything about it. I just did it." What I need to explain is that in Bethany you never heard the word "sex." No one talked about it and we never heard of it until we began to physically mature. It also probably explains why this did not traumatize LeRoy. He only thought of it as a normal procedure. The boys were not allowed to bath themselves. Each boy was bathed by the female member of the couple in charge of their cottage. In LeRoy's cottage, this woman paid special attention to cleaning their genitalia. After each boy was bathed, each one had to stand nude in the hall until they were all bathed. They then marched in line to the couple's bedroom where the man of the house stood nude. They paraded past him to the woman who again checked their genitalia "to be sure they were clean" and then the boys could go to bed. To me this was sexual abuse and repulsive. We all knew we were better off at Bethany than any other place, but we did not ask for this kind of behavior. At that time, LeRoy thought it was normal. When they got to bed they had to kneel by the bed and say their prayers before lights out.

After dinner, the support person took them to her room to read the Bible and she taught them what the readings meant. Religion was a big part of our lives. LeRoy was just there, but bored.

All the boys became members of one of two gangs. One was called the Blue gang and the other the Red. LeRoy was a member of the Red gang. He was assigned to that gang by the head of the Blue Gang. Since the Blue gang ruled the Red gang, the Red gang waited on the Blue gang and did things like combing their hair or shining their shoes. Whatever they were asked to do they were expected to obey. Seems neither group was harmful. It seemed more like a game. There was little physical fighting anywhere on the campus. One night the Red gang put on a show on the stage just for their cottage. LeRoy had planned to do something funny. Before he got the chance, the Blue gang made them get off the stage. LeRoy needed laughs and his big disappointment was not getting off the stage but not being able to deliver his funny lines to get the laughs. His whole life he wanted attention and he always set himself up to get it but in healthy and fun ways.

One night a member of the Blue gang came to him after lights out to ask him if he could keep a secret. LeRoy answered yes. The boy told him when the clock strikes 3AM, I am going to run away. Why he picked that time he never explained but he did leave exactly at 3. He was about 9 years old so it was a huge undertaking on his part because Bethany never took anyone back if they ran away. Very rarely did anyone even make the effort. Even as children, we knew Bethany was better for us than our families of origin even when we complained. Only two or three tried this in my fifteen years there. This kid later became LeRoy's brother-in-law.

All holidays were over-the-top. They all became big parties and something all of us looked forward to. For Halloween we went to school in the morning and as usual we went home for lunch. After lunch we would get dressed up in our costumes so we could go back to the school to celebrate and as we entered the building, we stopped for the teacher to guess who was under our costume. Bobbing apples was the big event where big vats of water were placed in our school rooms and we climbed up a few steps to reach the water and put our hands behind our backs and tried to nab an apple with our mouths. After that game we were given a candied apple for a treat. The only one we got all year.

LeRoy went back to his cottage for lunch one Halloween and was upset because he had no costume. The matron suggested he dress like Hitler and she made him up to look the part. It was a very untimely idea on the part of the matron. When he got to school the principal was furious. He took LeRoy into the library which we all knew meant a spanking. LeRoy protested that it was the matron's idea but to no avail. LeRoy got the royal spanking. What LeRoy was not privy to at that time was that the principal had just received a draft notice to report for active duty during the Second World War. It was early in the war when our government was still worried whether we could win in the Pacific due to the many gains the Japanese were making

LeRoy had turned 10 and it was time for him to go to the Administration Building. He packed up his belongings and walked to the building on his own. It was customary to leave without goodbyes to staff or to the other kids. Leaving was just another thing assigned to you and you did it.

CHAPTER 4:
ADMINISTRATION BUILDING

LeRoy walked about 20 steps to get into the main entrance. Straight ahead was the office of the superintendent. Immediately to the right was where our mail was delivered and where the secretary worked. As you passed that room, to the right was a long hall with two additional rooms. They both were used as a school for special education kids. Our principal was a Phi Beta Kappa and started this special education program long before most people ever heard of them. At the other end of the hall to the left of the office was the financial officer and next to him was a candy store, which existed until the dentist got so tired of being overwhelmed with our cavities that he arranged to have it closed. To the right was a big staircase that led to the boy's quarters. They had three bedrooms for the sixty boys housed there. One was for the younger boys and one for the older boys. In between was the bedwetters' room. LeRoy said it was always smelly.

Beyond the steps and to the left was a long breezeway which housed the chapel. Everyone on the campus had to go to services every single night. The boys sat on one side of the aisle and the girls on the other and God forbid if we talked to the opposite sex even if we had siblings in the same room. In fact, by this time most of us did not look for our siblings. LeRoy has no memory of looking for me nor I of him.

Beyond the breezeway was the girls' side which contained the main kitchen where all the food was prepared for the whole campus. A big dining room was across from the kitchen and the fifty boys and fifty girls ate their meals separated by a wide aisle where the matrons patrolled to be sure no one would trespass to the wrong side. Food was served family style with the girls setting the table, the cook filling bowls, and the girls taking them to the tables - even to the boys' side. We could ask for seconds but that was not always easy because at the same time they were encouraging us to hurry so we could get to our work or school. We came back to our cottages every day for lunch. The boys marched in from their side of the building and entered from a different doorway. When their meal was over, they marched back to their quarters.

After breakfast, the younger boys had to walk around the grounds armed with buckets to pick up all trash they found. Seasonal work was trimming hedges and mowing lawns under the supervision of the man who was a six day a week gardener and lived on campus with his family. The older boys went to the farm.

While LeRoy was one of the younger boys, he also had to check a blackboard on the wall to ascertain what his individual chores were. One day he looked to see what was expected of him and when he saw what was posted he felt overwhelmed and sat under the board and started to cry. The matron saw him crying. She inquired as to why was he crying. He told her it was too much work and he could never do it all. She told him that in the 15 minutes he had been there crying, he could be half finished. That stuck with him and he heard that replayed in his head for the rest of his life. I can attest to the fact he never shirked any task as an adult. In fact, he probably took on more than what most people could do.

On Saturdays, it was posted on the board whether you earned merits or demerits throughout the week and what the rationale was for the decisions. Your allowance was based on that record. Each cottage took their allowance to the candy store that day at a designated time to purchase candy. LeRoy recalls that he seldom got to the candy store for he had too many demerits based on minor infractions. It did not take much to get a demerit. He recalls getting quite a few for talking back to a matron. He got his only merit for saying good morning to her but since he never was much of a candy eater, it was not a big deal to lose that privilege. For most of us that was such a treat and our behavior reflected that.

In wintertime the older boys plowed the snow with a plow they called "The Winter Plow." It was an old wooden mule plow which took at least twelve boys sitting on it to hold the plow to the ground. If they did not sit on it, the blade that plowed flew up in the air and it was unable to do the job. Thank goodness they now own modern ones.

The usual weekly chores did not apply to Saturday or Sunday. The boys darned socks on Saturday morning and then they were free for the day. Sunday we all went to Sunday school after breakfast, church after lunch, and chapel in the evening. Dinner was served at 5PM with chapel at 7PM. Sunday was a boring day but after church we sneaked off-campus listening for the big campus clock that could be heard a mile away to tell us when to return so we could be there in time for a meal (where an empty space was easily detected). We knew enough to get back before the stroke of 5. Church was over at three so that gave us 2 hours to get into trouble, which LeRoy managed to do quite often.

One day while LeRoy was walking to the dining room, he found a screw on the ground and he asked one of the other boys if they wanted a screw and it was overheard by the matron. Finding something was like finding a treasure. To offer it to someone was a special treat. She told him he had to darn extra socks for saying a bad thing. He knew nothing about sex, so he had no idea why he needed to be punished. It would not have been

Institutionalized and Happy

encouraged to question her. When he told me he darned socks I was confused. I thought the girls did all the darning because we used to complain to each other that we thought the boys should be doing their own socks. Only now as I write this did I learn that they too were doing it.

Bethany being at the foot of the mountain, the woods were an interesting place to visit even though they were off-limits. LeRoy spent a great deal of time there both legitimately and illegitimately. The woods offered solace and fun. We all knew where the Initial tree was located, and we all wanted our names on it, as had been done for years by "former kids" as we called them. LeRoy and his friends had to climb the tree to find a space to put their names. It was so full. Nearby was a tree we all called the "lonely pine" as it was the only conifer in the woods. Many times, LeRoy visited these trees with other guys to sit and talk. He has no memory of the content of those conversations but he remembers how much he enjoyed just "bull crapping." I might add, these trees were almost sacred to us and everyone on campus was in awe of them. I suspect the staff did not know them, and what could have been more enticing to us then to have a big secret from staff?

In another section of the woods was a lake which had many trees around it. LeRoy and his friends would often find a liana and swing across the lake. They named it the Blue Lake and they felt like little Tarzans. One day a boy broke his leg and another boy carried him half a mile to the infirmary. These boys were only about 11 at that time. The nurse was such a caring person and was able to get the doctor to come from the town to fix him up post-haste. Although we were all emotionally deprived kids, the boys never had serious fights among themselves. They were concerned about one another. It was not stated but understood. They certainly never told each other how they felt about anything. Yet, concern comes out of feelings. They just quietly hurt or were angry. They were all in this together and it was the boys versus the staff. Matrons eyes seemed to follow them wherever they were. No wonder they stuck together.

Our reservoir was in the same area of the woods with huge ant hills to the right. LeRoy and his friends dug sticks into these tall foot-high red ant hills until they would begin to bite. I can attest to their bite being harsh! If it was hot and we were thirsty there was a place on the reservoir wall where the water seeped out. That was the most refreshing and pure water!

We called the top of the mountain Eagles Peak. LeRoy and his pals made sling shots with wood they found, using pieces of inner tubes as the band. They stayed at Eagles Peak for hours shooting rocks down the mountain. Any kind of sport was his thing and still is today. He is still as competitive as ever but remains a good sport and never fails to congratulate winners.

There was a quarry in the mountains that took rocks, put them in cable cars overhead, and shipped them over heavy cables to a town near Womelsdorf called Newmanstown. We girls ran to get under these cables quickly because we were afraid they would break when a car was overhead. LeRoy went up there to watch the process, which he felt was a fun outing. That was also off-limits, but he loved to explore and travel.

Between the woods and the baby cottage was a big area we called the dirt heap. Apparently, hunters came through the woods, but they rarely saw them. They felt alone there. We never saw wildlife except maybe a rabbit or two. There must have been deer but we never saw them.

LeRoy and his friends occasionally found empty bullet shells in the dirt heap near the baby cottage. They would fill them with firecrackers, seal them, and then set them on fire to hear the noise they made. The thrill was hearing the "pop" to know they had been successful. LeRoy was certainly now a thinking boy and was able to create when the need was apparent.

Bedtime was quite a time. The boys had to wear nightgowns and when they were ready for bed they had to kneel on the bed and pull their nighties up to their waists while the female matron walked by each of them and looked at their genitalia. This was similar to the abuse he experienced in Knerr Cottage, but at the time LeRoy never gave it a thought. Again, he was just there doing the robotic, obedient thing. This dormitory housed about 60 boys. It was the older boys' side that had to do this awful thing and they were 12 to 13 years old. It had to be humiliating for those who understood, but not to LeRoy. He was so into burying his feelings that he said, "I just did what they told me to do." Awful! Each night before bed they knelt by their beds and said their prayers. What hypocrites this "Christian" couple were. The man was eventually fired for beating up one of the older boys.

LeRoy slept next to the door and got himself dressed first so he could go around and wake up the other boys in all three dorms by ringing a bell. Whoever was chosen to ring the bell also had to walk the length of the campus every day at 4pm to pick up the mail from the train station - even in rain, snow, or sleet. Bethany seemed to know all of us well and could decide which child was the most responsible.

We were reminded many times about Jesus and how much we should be like him. LeRoy and I both think this was not a bad idea. We differ in our religious faith but we agree with Bethany that Jesus is a good example to follow. I have become an atheist while he is a devout Christian and goes to church every Sunday.

Some of the infractions we were punished for were such small wrongdoings. We were rarely able to defend ourselves. It was their word against ours and they were always right. One time LeRoy was a radio announcer at a chapel service, and he said it was *about* 4 minutes to 8. The superintendent went out of his way to tell LeRoy," It is either 4 minutes to 8 or it isn't. Which is it?" They could not let us get out of their system where everything had to be perfect. Too much was at stake for them.

He found a box of metal nuts one day and thought they would be fun to shoot. He had a great time shooting them with his homemade slingshot, but the principal saw him and told him he had to be punished for what he had done. He had to get down on his knees and kick his feet into the air for a half hour. I always felt LeRoy was not one of the principal's favorites. That certainly was an excessive punishment if a punishment was necessary. I was so disappointed to learn this because I loved the principal and he was so good to me. I got oodles of good healthy fathering from him. I saw his faults but they were not applied to me. I heard other stories about him that were not so nurturing, yet I dearly loved him and regret I never got to tell him how he influenced my life and still does.

Every Friday night we looked forward to homemade ice cream. LeRoy helped the staff make enough for all the staff as well as the 287 children. It was made with the whole milk from our farm with peaches and other fruit. The one we girls liked the least was banana because it was made with banana extract. All the other flavors were wonderfully delicious. Bethany worked hard to treat us in so many ways and they succeeded. Each treat was such a high for us and we were delighted with all of them.

LeRoy was still robotic in all his chores but was rebellious outside of that routine. We were all bodies in a well-orchestrated system that had no tolerance for emotions or attachments. We girls thought we were overworked but now I think it was worse for the boys. They had to do dangerous tasks and I am shocked there were not more accidents. In fact, there were very few. Most tasks were closely supervised.

Another chore he had to do was all the laundry for about 60 boys in two of the dorms. The winter was the pits for him as he had to hang the clothes outside to dry. It doesn't make sense to me because right next door was a commercial washer and dryer which we girls used. We never hung our clothes outside. We used a huge scary mangle to iron all the bed linens for the whole campus but we were never out in the cold just to hang up clothing.

Anniversary Day, celebrated on the anniversary of the founding of Bethany, was an over-the-top affair. A humungous tent was put up and wares of all kinds were available under it, such as handmade crafts, homemade soups made by churches that supported Bethany, lots of candy, and other snack foods. We children put on a religious pageant where hundreds of people flocked to the grove to watch us perform. Someone was hired to sew for weeks to make our costumes. The Ringgold Band would come from Reading and play all the Sousa marches and other music. Dinners were served in 4 cottages and were also run by the churches. Everything cost money but we were each given $5 to spend. LeRoy does not remember ever receiving this $5. Could it be because he misbehaved? No work was required of us on that day and we were set free to wander the campus. None of us would have thought to leave because what could be better than Anniversary Day? This was also the biggest fundraiser of the year for Bethany.

On one anniversary, LeRoy's matron told him to go to the "bubblers" (water fountains connected to our nearby spring house) because his mother was there. LeRoy was not expecting to see her and this was the first time he had seen her since we were admitted to Bethany 6 years ago. He was then 11 years old. He approached the bubblers and saw there were about 4 women there and he wondered which one was his mother, so he announced his name and said he was looking for his mother. How sad that is! She spoke up and said she was his mother. LeRoy first noticed she had on a pair of men's shoes and an ugly house dress. She did not look like a happy person. They talked a little, but he has no idea what they talked about. She wanted to walk up to the big tent. LeRoy agreed to go and when they arrived, she bought a dime's worth of coconut strips. They returned to the bubblers where she proceeded to eat all of them without offering LeRoy a single bite. Meanwhile, I was walking close by and per chance saw the two of them together and I knew her right away. I walked down and saw what she looked like and then and there I knew I would never be like her. Before that, I idolized her as almost a fairy godmother and knew she had not been to visit because she was busy. What a shock for me to see how poor she apparently was. I walked away and LeRoy and I did not speak. We left her sitting there alone. It was a horrible experience for both of us. We wonder why nobody let us know she was coming or why she didn't write to tell us she was coming. She probably picked that day because it was such a party day for everyone who participated in it. LeRoy went back to the dorm when the day was over, and our older brother Sam presented him with a lovely blue shirt which he said our mother told him to give to LeRoy. He was so proud and cherished it because he had never gotten any present from her. Looking back, it almost sounds like a substitute for the silk petticoat. He only had it a short time before the matron came in and began twisting his ear. She said that the shirt was stolen and she wanted it back. Sam had stolen it and our mother had nothing to do with it. LeRoy was totally crushed but gave it back. This was only the first thing that Sam did to LeRoy to hurt him.

When the boys went to bed and all was quiet, he and a friend would put a chair about 2" from the transom and crawl to the other side. They snuck down to the first floor, went into the treasurer's office and stole the keys to the candy store. They would eat some, but money was their goal. They never got any. Then they would go to the superintendent's office and look around but did not touch anything and then back to bed. They were never caught. Bethany did not have security guards but they didn't need them. Staff was always on top of us and if we were up to no good it felt like they could smell it.

LeRoy now turned 13 and it was time for him to go to the oldest boy's cottage. He packed up his clothes and off he went to Dietrich.

CHAPTER 5: DIETRICH

LEROY WAS SHOWN HIS BED and the kitchen and went directly to dinner as it was the custom to arrive at that time.

His first jobs in Dietrich were to assist in the kitchen. Setting the tables and drying dishes was not a simple task because 25 boys and a couple resided there. There were no dishwashers on the campus except in the main kitchen. After some of the other jobs he had in the past, these were easy.

One day as he walked into the kitchen, he saw a beautiful apple pie. Next to it sat a bottle of vanilla. "Wow, what a treat!" he thought. He picked up the vanilla and gulped it down. It tasted horrible. He still doesn't eat apple pie even though he knows it was the vanilla and that there is no logic to his thinking.

Soon younger boys came to the cottage so LeRoy got assigned to the farm. They sat on stools to milk all of the cows except for Rosie. Rosie's udders hung to the ground because her job was to produce calves. LeRoy sat on the floor to milk her because her udders hung so low. He loved Rosie and he greeted her each morning. One bull impregnated all the cows. How busy that bull was because there were 30 cows. LeRoy took care of the calves which I thought would have been fun, but he says he just did his job whether it was fun or not.

His jobs varied according to the season or the needs for the day and the changes were welcomed. His spring job was to spread manure with a plow on all the gardens, and we had many. He collected all the chickens' eggs and took them to the main kitchen for washing, crating, and distributing around the campus. It was a long walk from the chicken coops to the main kitchen. I am beginning to wonder how any of us had time for school.

The worst task he had was to kill stray cats by hitting them over the head then throwing them in the manure pile. There were just too many on the farm and Bethany could not afford to feed them with a full population of children. When I asked him how he felt about doing such a grotesque job, he said, "It was my job." Again, it is amazing to me the young ages at which these boys did men's work. Sometimes he drove a tractor with an electric thresher or a baler behind it to gather wheat for the cattle's winter food. We don't remember one boy who became a farmer after they left Bethany.

This was a phenomenon I had never heard of. LeRoy took celery he harvested to the main kitchen, and if they had extra, LeRoy dug a hole to bury them for the winter until the main kitchen requested them. Who would have thought you could do that? He also picked corn, husking it right on the field if they had the time to husk. Otherwise, it was shipped to the main kitchen and the girls husked it. I always thought we were the only huskers and we felt we were husking for a thousand people we did so many cobs.

LeRoy seemed to enjoy getting into trouble. He always did his jobs, but his free time was not well-used. I never figured out what he was doing wrong but through the grapevine I knew he was often in trouble. The things he did (like giving matrons a hard time) were not gross, but deviated enough from the system to cause him problems.

For instance, he and a friend went up to the mountains to explore. They came across a store they had never seen before and decided they wanted to rob it the next week. The day came to do this nasty thing and when they got into the mountains, they lost track of the store's location, so they were unable to commit the robbery. If they had done it and were caught Bethany would have thrown them out. As they were walking back, they came across a truck belonging to a hunter. They looked inside and saw his lunch and stole it. They ate it and were fascinated by the fact that it was a bean sandwich. They never had a bean sandwich and LeRoy was intrigued by it. He said it was delicious and can still taste it today.

Movies in the neighboring town of Robesonia were so exciting. They carried the latest shows and on a school night when the theater was almost empty the owner let a bus load of us come to his theater for free. He was wonderful to allow this. One week the boys went and the girls the next. Bethany arranged many social trips outside of the campus and it helped to get our minds off of our family problems. LeRoy missed many of the events offered to us because your ability to participate depended on your behavior. He didn't share specifics with me but I know some and they don't seem so bad.

Another exhilarating event was to go to Hershey Park with $5 from Bethany to ride the rides. We caught the train at the base of the campus and from the train we could walk to the park. The smell of Hershey in those days was delicious. That was before they made ecological changes. The town reeked of chocolate and we wallowed in that lovely smell and taste. Their chocolate milk was beyond description. Much better than today's. LeRoy never got there because of his behavior. Treats like this kept many of us obedient, but not LeRoy.

At night he sometimes snuck back to the barn to ride the mules bareback in great ecstasy, imagining himself a real cowboy. What fun he had, but they were never meant for riding and now he wonders what would have happened if he got hurt with no one around to help him.

If he had fallen and been badly hurt, I know from experience what happens to a deprived child under such trying circumstances. It is like you are in a trench and the enemy is all around you. You have no parental images or comforting people to conjure up and you feel emotionally alone. I think of a song we sang in elementary school which always brought tears to my eyes. It started like this, "Just before the battle mother, I am thinking most of you." We have no images. My therapist told me that this is what they call PTSD in military language. We have only ourselves. No one is behind us. The younger you are when you face abandonment, the harder it is to emotionally grow.

LeRoy was always a competitive person and loved sports even though we were not allowed to form competitive teams. He played any sport any time he had the opportunity, and was a good sport even if he lost but he mostly won. He competed only with himself. He was with a group of boys one day and they decided to burn railroad ties. One boy challenged LeRoy to walk across the burning ties. You could not challenge LeRoy because he bit every time. He did do it, and put on his best happy face, but once he was out of view of the other boys, he ran up to his cottage crying all the way. He never told the other boys what had happened nor did he tell any adult. He was a brave soul and proud of it. For the rest of his life his goal was to accumulate as many medals as he could. He won many throughout his life, but never bragged about them. He stored them in his basement and only people he chose to take down to see them ever knew this about him. They seemed to be the nurturing he missed as a child and he got plenty of it through sports. Again, he was always looking for attention in healthy (and mischievous!) ways and always figured out how to do that.

We were not allowed pets, but LeRoy found a stray dog while roaming in the mountains. He and a friend made a house for it. They would take soda bottles to a store at a rebate rate of two cents per bottle. If they had quart size bottles, they got a nickel for each. That money went for dog biscuits which they walked about two miles to buy them. On the way back to the mountains to feed the dog, the two of them often ate half of them. The dog was always there to receive them and enjoyed the other half. How yucky to eat that stuff!

LeRoy graduated from the eighth grade at 15 years of age. He did well in school, with mathematics and history as his strengths. There was no party or any recognition for graduates. No congratulations or goodbyes, students were just dismissed as usual.

When he got back to his cottage, he and two other graduates were told to pack up their clothes and go to the superintendent's office, which they did. The superintendent informed them that they were going to leave Bethany permanently and that they were going together to a place called Steven's Trade School. This was a school where they were to learn a skill which would set them up for a lifetime of employment. They were driven to their new home in the Bethany bus. I was astounded at the abruptness of his leaving. I was not told he had gone, which was the normal practice. We found these kinds of things out through the grapevine. That's how I knew he was a troublemaker but I never heard what he had done. All he remembers of me was seeing me one day when I was 6 walking to school. He doesn't know why that made such a big impression, but he thinks of it as a nice memory. We both feel we had some kind of connection before Bethany because every time anything nice happens to me he reminds me of that day. It was through the grapevine that I found out he had left Bethany forever. I need to digress to tell you about his school years at Bethany. Then we will move on to the rest of his life.

CHAPTER 6:
LEROY'S SCHOOL DAYS AT BETHANY

KINDERGARTEN WAS HELD IN LEINBACH COTTAGE where I lived, next to Frick where LeRoy was living. He has no memories of that school year except that he flunked. The story they told him was that he was not hearing well so he couldn't speak correctly. If they flunked him, he would learn to speak correctly and then he would hear in a normal fashion. Of course, that did not work because he was tongue tied which no one seemed to pick up on. He needed surgery so his second year did not take care of the problem either.

Most of his school days are a blur to him. He has blocked out his first three years and remembers little of them. The principal was wonderful to me but I believe he was not too fond of LeRoy because he thought LeRoy was deliberately speaking in the manner he did. He thought it was some type of rebellious behavior. Rebellion was not his style. He was too transparent to rebel.

In 4th grade he participated with his class in a big day on campus called May Day. Every class had to do some creative act in an open space on the campus attended by all eight classes. Staff was not there to see what their kids were doing. Now that seems terrible. The day terminated with a maypole dance with the eighth-grade girls dancing in their white attire. His act that year was to repeat with his whole class this little poem. Who knows what the significance of it was then or even now. It is a very strange ditty. It goes like this:

Are you ready for the fight?

Yes, I am ready for the fight

Cause we are the Roman soldiers.

There you have it. No one wore costumes except the Maypole Dancers so the poem made little sense. It also was so incongruent with Bethany's basic philosophy which was to always be kind.

In 4th grade LeRoy did well in school so the teacher told him he should become a math teacher as he excelled above his classmates. This never materialized.

In fifth grade he was driven to Reading every Wednesday night and while the treasurer picked up oysters for staff, LeRoy waited for him for half an hour in a closed telephone booth repeating three words to practice his speaking. They were "store, door, and Miss Hefelfinger," his teacher's name. He did this for 3 years and his speech remained the same. He was blamed for his speaking problem but what a waste of time those trips were for him. It did get him off campus and out of work, though.

All holidays at Bethany were over-the-top. They were big parties and all of us looked forward to them. On Halloween we had our morning classes and, as usual, went to our cottages for lunch. After lunch we got dressed up in our costumes so we could go back to the school to celebrate. We went back to school with our teachers standing outside of the door waiting to guess which one of us was under each costume. After we had all taken our seats, the thrill was to climb up a few steps to a huge vat filled with water and apples floating all around. We put our hands behind our backs and tried to nab an apple with our teeth. It was a sloppy and messy time but such fun with a reward at the end of the afternoon of a candied apple. The only one we got all year. We thought they were the most delicious treat ever.

LeRoy went back to his cottage for lunch one Halloween and was upset because he had no costume. The matron suggested he dress like Hitler and she made him up to look the part. It was a very untimely idea on the part of the matron. When he got to school the principal was furious. He took LeRoy into the library which we all knew meant a spanking. LeRoy protested that it was the matron's idea but to no avail. LeRoy got the royal spanking. What LeRoy was not privy to at that time was that the principal had just received a draft notice to report for active duty during the Second World War. It was early in the war when our government was still worried whether we could win in the Pacific due to the many gains the Japanese were making. Ultimately, he was excused from service because of his job, but he didn't know that on Halloween.

5th through 8th grade had study hours at 8PM every school night. This was when we did our homework or asked the teacher in charge any questions we had about our work. We were not allowed to visit unless we could prove we were talking about homework. 8th graders had to be available to 7th graders and help them with their questions. LeRoy was answering a question for a 7th grade girl and the teacher came along and pulled his ear for giving her a wrong answer. He had to do exercises for her the next day for what she deemed a mistake. To this day, LeRoy thinks he was right.

We both remember when Sam was in the 8th grade, he had apparently come to school a little disheveled and unclean. The principal opened the sliding doors which divided the large upstairs room into one room instead of two. Each half of the room housed two grades so opening the door exposed fifth grade through eighth grades. LeRoy and I were both witnessed the principal with a big tub of water as he proceeded to have Sam strip to the waist and washed him. Both LeRoy and I felt humiliated and sad for Sam. We were not close to Sam and barely knew him but still recognized that he was our brother. I guess it is true that blood runs thicker than water because we never did get close to Sam although LeRoy tried hard to stay in touch and did from time to time.

It was time to graduate from 8th grade and the principal told LeRoy he wouldn't graduate unless he learned to speak properly. LeRoy never thought he talked differently from anyone so his speech was never an issue for him. He was called to the infirmary to see a young doctor Bethany had hired to take care of his problem since the old doctor had retired. This doctor saw the problem immediately and told him to open his mouth and he snipped something under his tongue with no anesthesia or any warning as to what he was going to do. LeRoy was no longer tongue-tied. What a change it made, as he often had to give speeches later in his life. We suspect the old doctor just did not understand the problem. What a terrible thing to base one's graduation upon. Not to mention that being tongue-tied had previously caused LeRoy to flunk kindergarten. He suffered for all those years with something so easy to fix. LeRoy said everyone had told him he talked "funny" but he thought he sounded like everyone else. That is astounding to me! He would pronounce his name as "Nenoy." Recently, LeRoy called Sam, who now has dementia and asked him if he knew who he was talking to and Sam said, "Yes. It's Nenoy." It is surprising what Sam remembers at 94.

LeRoy did graduate and left for the cottage, as there was no ceremony nor goodbyes. It just was. When he got back to the cottage he and a couple other boys were told to pack up their belongings and report to the superintendent's office. He had no knowledge, nor did the others, as to what was going to happen. The boys were surprised to find out they were going to leave Bethany permanently and go to a school in Lancaster, Pennsylvania called Stephen's Trade School to learn a trade. They were driven there in Bethany's bus and dumped off.

CHAPTER 7:
TRADE SCHOOL AND HIS FIRST HOME

LEROY WAS HAPPY AND COMFORTABLE, and not lonely with a few other Bethany boys with him. They toured the campus grounds and were shown the dormitories by one of the residents, then had dinner. The rules of conduct were somewhat like a military school. For example, the upper classmates walked on the sidewalk and the newbies had to walk on the street if they passed them. LeRoy smiled every time he had to go on the street and became known as Smiling Jack. The next day, as part of their initiation they sat in an electric chair and current was shot through it. It upset the staff when they found out and the chair was deliberately broken the next day. Then they were tarred and feathered. The tar was spread on their faces and then feathers thrown at them to stick to the tar. The tar was almost impossible to wash off. LeRoy thought it was fun and had "nothing to complain about." They also had to roll a peanut down their quarter mile driveway with their noses while staff watched and laughed. How could staff condone such nonsense?

His first job was to work in a shop making center points. When a nail was pounded into a piece of wood, the center point was used to secure the nail in the wood. He did this for three months and was bored to tears making them so he decided to run away, leaving his friends behind. Bethany would not take anyone back after they were discharged. He hitchhiked to Reading and arrived at our mother's apartment where she lived with our older brother, Sam, and her common-law husband Calhoun. In Pennsylvania at that time if you lived together for seven years, you were legally married. LeRoy had no funds so that was the only place he could afford. He was accepted for the possibility of more income for our mother and her husband who would charge him room and board. Sam could not afford to pay for both guys even though he was always generous with his money. Sam worked at a grocery store, Cassells. LeRoy hoped he could get a job there too. Sam convinced him he should go to Reading High School to continue his schooling and work part-time, as he did. He could walk to the grocery store so it worked out well for him. When I asked him how he felt living with his mother he said it was all right. Our mother was just there and her common law husband was not a man he liked right off the bat. He stayed because he could not afford to live anywhere else.

LeRoy, our mother, LeRoy's son, Walter, and Walter's son.

He continued to go Bethany every weekend to see his sweetheart Wray, who would later become his wife. They were partners in whatever LeRoy wanted to do. I cannot imagine how they were never caught because he was not supposed to be there without

Institutionalized and Happy

permission from the superintendent. Incidentally, I was still at Bethany and I never knew LeRoy was visiting because he never came to see me, nor did he attempt to. He was too much in love to look me up as I was in a different building than Wray's.

At Reading High School he was doing fine and when his teacher found out he was raised at Bethany she had him speak to the class about his experiences there. He was not satisfied with continuing his schooling because he wanted more income so he quit before finishing 10th grade and never went back. He immediately went to work at Cassells fulltime where he was earning a quarter an hour. Although he wanted better pay, he never thought of looking for other employment. He was always true to employers whether it made sense or not. He just did his job.

Sam nor LeRoy got along with Calhoun. All of us called him Calhoun, his last name, because none of us could stand him. Sam was more compliant than LeRoy so he made himself get along with him but LeRoy spoke up, which Calhoun could not handle. Calhoun thought of himself as someone above most people because he had an engineering degree. One day he challenged LeRoy to a fight and LeRoy said, "Come into the alley and I will beat the hell out of you." Our mom encouraged her husband to go, but the fight never occurred. LeRoy feels Calhoun knew he would lose and that our mother was cheering for LeRoy. LeRoy hoped that meant she had some concern for him.

He remembers our mother cooking and watching wrestling on TV, but they never interacted much. No one in the apartment seemed to converse. Calhoun sat in the front room with a typewriter at a window to make it look like he was working, although he was not. Whatever his problem was he was not a steady worker. He had an engineering degree and for a time worked for the city of Reading as an engineer, but he collected unemployment most of the time.

In about 1946 Cassells moved their store and LeRoy moved to a room close to the store so he would not have transportation expenses. He also wanted to get out of Calhoun's place. Meanwhile, every weekend he was still going to Bethany to visit Wray. Our mother ran a debit account at Cassells and before he left, Cassells tried to get LeRoy to pay it. He refused and he has no idea how it got paid, if it did.

Our mother moved from place to place but LeRoy kept track of all these moves from the time he left her house and he managed to keep in touch with her when he felt he had the time. He was the only one of us who kept in touch and when I asked him why, he said he did it because he felt obligated and it was just the right thing to do. He would have her for dinner occasionally. His kids would say, "Give grandmother a piece of cake and a cup of coffee and she is happy." One night he went to visit her with one of his children and she was living with a Mr. Zettlemoyer with both of their names on their door. LeRoy thought it was bad for his children to see that they were living together while unmarried so he told his mom that if they would go to Elkton, Maryland and get married, he would spring for the trip. They accepted his offer and he gave them $50. Our mother was so lucky. For the first time in her life, she found a man who loved and cared for her and they stayed together until he died. She never married or lived with a man again.

Wray had labor pains with one of her children (Jay) and needed a babysitter to get dinner for the kids. She was boiling potatoes to make mashed potatoes on the stove and called our mom to ask for her help. Wray told our mom about the potatoes and asked her to mash them. The kids wouldn't eat them because she put the pot on the table full of boiling water. We have no idea if she knew what she was doing or maybe she never made mashed potatoes. One of her favorite meals was baked lima beans which she served every Sunday to LeRoy and Sam when they lived together.

Institutionalized and Happy

LeRoy asked her to babysit another time (for the last time). Her response was, "I raised my kids so now you raise yours." LeRoy was shocked because she had 3 Calhoun children after us and she didn't raise them either. This did not deter LeRoy from maintaining that relationship.

She developed some health problems and was hospitalized in 1990. LeRoy saw her every day because he knew she was dying. One day our sister came to see her and they hadn't seen each other for years. She told someone in the room to get her out of there. Pearl left and when she told me I ached for her. I knew she craved a mother's love all of her life. Our mother clearly disliked her and no one knows why. LeRoy told me she was dying and asked me if I wanted to come to see her for the last time. I said no, which I still regret. I would have liked to tell her we forgave all she was unable to do for us. She asked LeRoy on one of her last days to hold her hand and he was happy to. She told him he was her favorite child. LeRoy thought that was a terrible thing to say but none of us cared, as LeRoy was the only one involved with her. She barely knew the rest of us.

She was 87 when she died and all the Gensemer children were at the funeral. What a shock when I saw the site of the burial and the coffin. It was a lovely site at the foot of a hill and the coffin was a coffin any middleclass family would have bought. She looked lovely in her coffin and probably better than she ever looked in her life. Pearl came to me and told me she bought the lovely gown she had on. I felt Pearl still was asking for mommy to love her. I asked LeRoy who paid for the funeral. He said, "mom did." She had an insurance policy just to cover a proper funeral. She wanted a procession and people to be gathered around and she got that too with her five Gensemer children and all of LeRoy's family. Sam refused to get involved with anything pertaining to her throughout her whole life. She always wanted a nice lifestyle and in death she got it. I asked the minister what he could say to a woman who wasted away a life. "She had you" was his response, and a lovely one at that. He could not have said anything better to me. Yes, she had given me life.

On LeRoy's first vacation from Cassells, he hitchhiked to Easton and was picked up by a man who offered to buy him a meal. LeRoy, true to form, accepted the offer. He asked LeRoy how he would like to go to New York. LeRoy thought that was a good idea so that became the plan. It was getting late and he asked LeRoy if he would stay at a motel and head to New York in the morning and LeRoy agreed. They got one room with one bed. LeRoy had no idea what was going to occur and when the pass came he told the man, "I'm not into that." The man left him alone and they had breakfast together, but as you could probably guess, LeRoy "let" the man pay. They headed for New York and when they arrived, he left LeRoy off near a policeman. He asked the policeman where he could stand to get a quick ride to Reading. The policeman showed him and he got a ride almost immediately. Two men picked him up and he was frightened because he thought they looked like gangsters. They drove him to a club in New Jersey and gave him five dollars. LeRoy left Reading with $8 and came back with $13. Typical LeRoy!

At Cassells LeRoy had to talk to customers and discovered that he liked people and wanted them to like him. He was generally liked and he learned to become outgoing and quite a conversationalist which put him in good stead for his future endeavors. Eventually, Cassells closed and LeRoy had to find another job. He found one in The White House Market in Mt. Penn, outside of Reading, where he found himself in a unique position. The store was owned by the Minker brothers, who were part of the Mafia in Reading and connected to the Philadelphia and New York mafia. Issy and Abe primarily ran the store, which they were as interested in as they were in the numbers business. LeRoy was hired to work in the dairy department with a supervisor who LeRoy thought was not worth his salt. They got along like oil and water. LeRoy reported his situation to Issy and Issy told him he would put LeRoy in the supervisor's position, which he did.

All cheese was sold from a wheel and when you bought cheese it was cut in a wedge. LeRoy got the idea that they might sell more if they cut it into bars and cubes. The idea took off quickly and they sold more cheese than ever before. Issy got a call from a Philadelphia man who ran one of the biggest grocery businesses in the city. He asked Issy to come down with LeRoy to talk about cheese. They were treated to lunch and then had a meeting to talk about what LeRoy was doing in his department. A few months later, the Philadelphia store came out with Cracker Barrel cheeses and Issy told LeRoy, "if I had known he was going to steal your idea, I would have sold it to him." LeRoy never got credit for it.

Issy wanted to open a Kosher deli and he asked LeRoy to visit a well-respected deli in Philadelphia with him. They drove down and LeRoy listened to all that was said and thought it a good idea for their market. Issy hired a Philadelphia man to set it up. There was only one other kosher store in Reading and it was quite busy. LeRoy ran Issy's kosher market and it was quite successful. One day the man who owned the Reading store asked Issy to buy him out because LeRoy was now doing better than the Reading store. Issy said, "why should I buy you out when LeRoy will put you out of business soon?" In fact, that is what happened.

Now the relationship between the Minkers and LeRoy was solid. They were driving LeRoy to work every day and buying him his weekly groceries, as LeRoy was still broke with a wife and six kids at home. They were generous about what he could buy. He also went to their homes to do maintenance work. They fully trusted LeRoy and LeRoy was loyal to them. He kept anything he knew about the basement activities to himself. He never shared his knowledge of the brothers, nor did he pry. They mutually respected each other and they trusted LeRoy more than anyone else who was outside of their numbers business. One

Easter Sunday Issy took LeRoy for his usual grocery shopping. He seemed unusually generous this time. On the way to LeRoy's house Issy asked him to become a driver for the numbers business. LeRoy declined and said he wouldn't do it because it was illegal. Issy said, "You son of a bitch. I buy you groceries every week and anyone else would be glad to do this for me." He dropped LeRoy home and went on his way. LeRoy dropped by a diner and a man they called Banana Joe stopped him and told LeRoy he heard he had turned Issy down for a job. He said to LeRoy, "You are now a dead man. No one says no to the Minkers." LeRoy went home scared to death. He changed his sleeping space every night for three nights. Then he got a call the next night to come up to Abe's house to hang a mirror. This petrified LeRoy and he told Wray he knew if he showed he would be killed, but he also knew they would get him eventually so he might as well go and get it over with. When he entered the house, Abe was walking down a hall toward him in the foyer with his hands in his pockets and LeRoy felt certain he had a gun with him. Abe came into the foyer, took his hands out of his pockets, and told LeRoy to shake his hand. As they shook hands Abe said to him, "You are the first man I know who is not out for my money," LeRoy hung the mirror and went home. I can only imagine the relief he felt, but they never bought him groceries again. After that incident, they often greased his palm with $50. It became obvious that they trusted him implicitly.

The market burned to the ground in 1956. They suspected a rival group of mobsters, but no one ever proved who did it. They asked LeRoy to ride up to the ruins and bring the safe with all the proceeds from the store in it. LeRoy told him he didn't own a car so they said, "Go get a cab and bring the money to my home. Don't let the driver touch it. You bring it." Of course, LeRoy did as he was told. They were so grateful they had him to trust. They wanted to rehire him when they rebuilt the grocery store so they asked him to be the security guard of the ruins. There was nothing to guard but LeRoy needed the cash so he did the job. They did eventually rebuild and LeRoy went back to work for them as the head of the dairy department.

Every Christmas the Minkers gave away turkeys, especially to politicians. LeRoy's job was to weigh all turkeys and charge 29 cents a pound for them. Abe bought the turkeys at 29 cents a pound but LeRoy made extra money by charging 39. One county commissioner came in and requested to watch LeRoy weigh the turkeys and saw he was charging 10 cents more per pound. The man complained to Abe. When the commissioner left, Abe said to LeRoy, "What the hell is he complaining about? He'll get one of ours for free." He was paying for that turkey, but Minkers were going to give him one for Christmas. The Minkers never chastised LeRoy. It wasn't nice for LeRoy to upcharge people, but he was still in a desperate financial position at that time.

These nefarious men trusted LeRoy completely. I was told the two things Mafia appreciate are authenticity and character - LeRoy had both. They admired him for his devotion to his family and his church. These were two areas where they were aligned with LeRoy's values. They even complimented him for having a conscience. Mafia have a reputation for great perception into a person's psyche. I guess that must come from the need to know who you can trust. I have no doubt that these men loved LeRoy. He saw them as father figures. With each of them valuing family and religion, the bond was strong. Mobsters are people too.

Eventually, a trashman found numbers in Abe's trashcan and reported him to the police. After he was released, he told LeRoy that he was free because of letters from his rabbi, a policeman, and LeRoy Gensemer. He was charitable to a hospital as well as to his synagogue and both hung plaques in his honor but they came down when he was jailed. He was the only one of the Minkers who served jail time. LeRoy felt bad about his being gone from the store during his sentence. I believe he acted as the father LeRoy never had. The trust and goodwill between them was strong. Both Minker brothers were devoted to the grocery business as was LeRoy which built a lot of respect between them.

Abe bought a beautiful apartment and told LeRoy to come see it. LeRoy did and was impressed. He made a special point of showing him his wife's walk-in closet jammed with clothes. Then he took him to his closet which had fewer clothes. He told LeRoy that is just the way it is.

Abe was on the phone with the Retailers' Union of which LeRoy was a member. LeRoy heard Abe call the man he was talking to "a son of a bitch." LeRoy told him to knock it off - that he couldn't talk to his fellow member like that. Abe said it again and LeRoy reiterated he should cut it out. He wouldn't stop so LeRoy reported him to the president of the union. Abe then said to LeRoy, "You son a bitch. You reported me to your union." LeRoy told him it wasn't right to talk to people like that. Abe never did it again.

Abe sent LeRoy to a Labor Council course for retailers on labor laws. He attended and at the end of the course he got a diploma which said he took and completed it at the University of Delaware. After that, LeRoy claimed that he 'attended' that university. He never said he graduated so he felt he was being honest. He used this line when he got into politics. His one regret in life was that he didn't have an education that he could be proud of.

LeRoy told Abe he had until Monday to come through with a raise he promised to his union workers. Abe's response was," I'll give you $400 for a new suit if you will forget the raise." LeRoy turned him down and Abe paid the bill of $58. Why was he so cheap in this instance? A few months later he did give LeRoy the $400 but it was not used for a suit.

At Christmas time LeRoy got a $300 bonus, but it was only given to him on Christmas Eve. That was too late for LeRoy to use to shop for his kids. He asked Abe if he could have it early. Abe always said yes and then he also gave LeRoy his usual $300 bonus on Christmas Eve. LeRoy tried to pay him back, but Abe always told him to forget it. This went on for most of his 17 years at the market. He sure had those guys wrapped around his finger but they knew it and liked it. No wonder LeRoy felt that he was their best friend.

After 17 years of working for them, the store closed permanently in 1968, as the Minker brothers were leaving for retirement in Florida. LeRoy missed them. He felt he lost two wonderful friends. He called Issy when he was in Florida for a union meeting and they had lunch together. It was a very lovely lunch and they talked about old times. He never saw any of them again. Now all five of them are dead.

He went to work in a steel plant where he had to straighten I-beams after they came off the assembly line. It earned him more money but he got bored after two years and joined the maintenance crew at Reading High School, where he worked for 21 years. During those days he became heavily involved in politics. He sometimes left his job at the school on his working hours to take care of political matters. He occasionally got caught, but because he had influence with the school board he never suffered any consequences. You will read more about that later.

Every time there was an event in the school stadium, LeRoy made sure he was the first one to clean under the bleachers so he could collect any money the kids dropped. He opened a bank account with this found money to see what amount he could collect by retirement age. It amounted to $800 after 21 years.

He had also opened a roofing business part-time while at the high school and his financial picture was much improved. He had the freedom to go out to dinner or see a movie any time he wanted, but was typically too busy doing charity work, politics, or roofing to take in any entertainment. Some of his children helped him if the work piled up. Bethany taught us to keep busy and LeRoy never forgot that and lived by it. "Just do it" was his motto. Wray told their children, "If you want to see your dad, you'll have to make an appointment."

In 1993 four teachers retired at the same time LeRoy had decided to and the school had one big ceremony for the five retirees, to recognize their service. They each received a check and LeRoy's was the biggest, which made him so proud. He was most appreciative of that recognition because he loved the positive attention and appreciation. He had earned it as well as his pension.

He went into the roofing business full-time and worked on individual houses as well as on the roofs in an apartment complex. So many family members were provided income through the business.

One day he took his son Brad with him to work on a woman's roof. When she saw the little boy, she was mortified and refused to have him go up the ladder. LeRoy finished the job and went to the lady's kitchen to pick up Brad. She told LeRoy how much she enjoyed his company and said, "You can bring him here any time. While you worked he told me your life's story."

He was roofing during WWII when people feared bombing here in the states and some people even built cement bomb shelters in their homes or backyards. LeRoy poured cement and built some of these structures. It was a while into the war before our country felt we would win. It was a very scary time.

For Christmas one year, Jay went to the apartment complex where his dad had the roofing contract. LeRoy was unable to go. Some man at the meeting made the comment that all politicians are crooks. Jay spoke right up and said, "Not my dad." LeRoy was so proud of him. He was right. LeRoy became known for his honesty all over Berks County through politics, which I will tell you about in another chapter. He was not in attendance at a school board meeting when they discussed who was the most honest politician they knew in Berks County. Unanimously, they named LeRoy. When this was later repeated to LeRoy, he told me it made him feel so good. There is that goal again. Get attention, but get it honestly.

Anytime my husband and I talked to LeRoy about his work he would tell us his prices. Whenever we told him he should be charging more, his answer was always, "I'm satisfied." He often charged little to poor families because he remembered when he was poor. He got propositioned one time in lieu of a payment, but he turned her down. If he was overwhelmed with work, he would get some of his boys to help him. He taught them the tarring part of the job and they became good at it. LeRoy would leave to do something else, but he went back to check each tarring job so all his customers were happy. If the job was a tall building he would call on our younger brother, who had a 60-foot ladder, to come work with him. He learned at Bethany that if you have a job to do and there is a problem, figure it. LeRoy learned that lesson well.

At this time, his home was in a neighborhood that was becoming unsafe and the kids were all out of the house so he moved to Exeter in 1994, not far from what had been the White House Market. He continued to work full-time as a roofer until one day an inspector for the county told him it was illegal to conduct business from a residential area. LeRoy told him the business was all in his truck in the driveway, but apparently that was still illegal. He then retired from the roofing business, but it wasn't in his character to sit and do nothing.

CHAPTER 8: POLITICS

IN 1964, WHEN LEROY WAS 47 YEARS OLD, married, and father of six children he was asked to help at the polls on election day. That was the beginning of a 50-year love affair in politics, which ultimately gave him so much satisfaction and pleasure. The first thing LeRoy discovered was that he would have to join the Allied Democratic Club. This was a club that extended over all of Berks County and all the other clubs in the districts and wards answered to this one. Every ward had clubs and each had officers headed by a president.

In 1973 he became the captain of the 17th ward, which was the biggest ward in Reading. That ward became a precinct and LeRoy was captain of that precinct. As captain he had to be certified to examine the polls to find out which Democrats had regularly voted. Then he went to the homes of those who had not voted to try to encourage them to get to the polls and vote.

He decided to run for vice president of the Allied Democratic Club while he still was involved with other clubs in other districts. He won that seat when he received 10 required signatures from the club and served from 1978-1980. It was only possible to run for one term of two years. If you wanted a seat in other wards you needed 150 votes. Often, he won those seats while he was holding offices in other wards so he had the responsibility of a few wards at one time. His jobs consisted of assisting the president, getting speakers for the club, having candidates come in to speak to the group, and informing the club

Institutionalized and Happy

members of what was happening in Berks county within the party. The club also helped the candidates plan and run their campaigns.

When his term as vice president was over, LeRoy decided he wanted to run for president. He found out that his competitor was a popular man who brought many people into the club to vote for him. LeRoy told the county commissioner that he would drop out of the race because he could see he was going to lose. The commissioner told him he could not drop out. He stayed in and won. It was a surprise win for everyone involved, but he wallowed to himself in his victory. One of the county commissioners called the Reading Times newspaper to announce LeRoy's victory but his opponent thought LeRoy had done it and chided him royally. Apparently, he found it hard to lose publicly. LeRoy was always happy to win but he never bragged about it nor did he tell too many people about his successes. Never did I know of all his accomplishments until writing this book, but if he felt it was an important win he called and he was proud to tell me. When his term was up in 1982, they changed the bylaws to say you could run for two consecutive terms because LeRoy was wanted to be the chair again. He worked for these clubs for 30 years with his eyes toward bigger things all along the way. President of the Allied Democratic Club was his next goal. He ran twice and won twice. You had to wait ten years between runs as president but they changed the bylaws so he could run consecutively. He was the first to hold that position for that long. These victories gave him the positive attention he craved. To say it another way, they were his source of nurturing.

The 17th ward held a dinner with LeRoy as their chairperson. It was up to him to be the speaker and to inform those who attended everything going on in the Democratic Party in all of Reading. That was his first major speech, and he was excited about how well it had gone. He was totally engrossed and committed to the party and never received any money for anything he did. The accolades and accomplishments were what he was after. The verbal thanks and praise were wonderful to receive but nothing was more important than the medals. They were long-lasting and proved his success to the world.

LeRoy also ran for prison inspector. When he ran for any office he paid all of his campaign expenses and never took money from anyone even if it was offered. During one of his prison inspector campaigns he collected empty soda cans, wrapped paper around them, and wrote on them: "You be the judge. Put LeRoy Gensemer in jail!" The first time he ran for this office he had to get his name out to the public. A man who ran a hotel called LeRoy and told him that if he dropped out of the race he would give him $400. LeRoy turned him down. He could never figure out why this occurred except he presumed it was a Minker because they knew that if LeRoy won there would be no favors, but he can't prove it. LeRoy was an unknown and as the new man on the block, he thought he had no chance of winning but he did. He ran three times and won each time. One of the times he ran, Issy Minker asked him to run with his girlfriend because there was more than one seat open. Leroy told him no because he wanted to make it on his own. He talked straight to Izzy and Abe and they respected that trait in him. He felt safe with them and they were always kind to him. I am amazed at their relationship.

Many times, there would be auctions to raise money for the Democratic Party. Each candidate was told to buy something. One of the commissioners always came to the auction with a cowboy hat. LeRoy took it off his head and auctioned it off. It sold for $12! When the auction was over he asked LeRoy what he should do to get his hat back. LeRoy said, "Go bargain for it." The commissioner walked out with it but LeRoy doesn't know what transpired between the buyer and the commissioner. He did the darndest things and got away with it.

He felt he now needed a business card, which he was able to get for free at the local high school. A union man found out and told him, "Unless you get your cards from us, we will not support you." LeRoy's response was, "No problem" and he got the union to make new ones. He just did it like he was supposed to.

Bethany had a newspaper called the Bethany Echo and it endorsed LeRoy every time he ran for any office. They were not only proud of their alum, and when I get to his career at Bethany in his older years, it will make sense they supported him.

As part of the job, LeRoy had to make unannounced inspection tours of the prisons. One day he was there with other inspectors and was suddenly pushed into a closet with the others. He had no idea what was happening but it turned out to be a prison riot. He was there for half an hour. He said he was relaxed and not frightened because he didn't know what was going on. One day, a prison guard was outside of the prison and exposed himself to the prisoners. He was immediately suspended until his case could be heard in court. The court found him guilty and he was fired. LeRoy was proud of the part he played in that case.

When he retired from prison inspector after serving three consecutive terms from 1966-1971, LeRoy decided to run for Jury Commissioner and won five terms. His slogan was "Drive safely. The vote you save might be for LeRoy Gensemer." He campaigned for the job consistently and wanted to run on his own so he accepted no help in all of his campaigns, including financial assistance. He went to a church one time and gave a campaign speech. He mentioned that three girls worked in the office. As he was leaving, the minister stopped him and said, "The people in the office are not girls, they are women. I won't vote for you." LeRoy said, "Not everyone loves LeRoy Gensemer but when Jesus was on this earth many people didn't like him." The minister smiled and said, "You got my vote." LeRoy had 13 posters to display and the minister took 12 of them.

When the judge swore him in, as was the custom, he said to LeRoy, I can't swear you in unless you pay me the $8 I paid for a can of tomatoes at your auction." Then he said, after the swearing in, that he hoped LeRoy would not give up his roofing business "for this f------ office." LeRoy was stunned. The judge asked if they had any questions and the woman who was also sworn in asked, "if someone asks me to fix a ticket, what should I do?" The judge answered, "Ask LeRoy because everyone knows LeRoy." Altogether, LeRoy served as Jury Commissioner from 1985-2005.

He was elected campaign manager of four wards and he drove 22 miles for every monthly meeting. Things were different than they are today. All candidates paid dues to the party to run for a seat, then the party helped them with their campaign. If the candidate lost their campaign, they did not get their money back. It stayed with the party. The candidates knew this rule before they participated, but things have changed since and this is no longer the case.

LeRoy started to interview candidates to see if they had any skeletons in their closet so there would be no surprises on the campaign trail that might disqualify them. A woman who was running came into LeRoy's office to be interviewed. They talked and he asked her if she had any skeletons in her closet and she said, "I went to Kutztown State College and I was the only woman who graduated a virgin and the Lord is my cornerstone." LeRoy told her if she wanted to get elected she would have to change her approach to the people. She refused and was never elected.

Another woman came to be interviewed for an office and LeRoy asked her if she had any skeletons in her closet. She said she had done pin cushioning but was no longer doing it. LeRoy asked her what that meant. She said she had slept around with men in Berks County but had quit doing it. She ran and lost. LeRoy's candidate won. For his own protection, he never interviewed a woman without his female secretary in the room.

The city controller asked LeRoy to accompany him to meetings in many of the wards. In fact, he wanted him at all the meetings. LeRoy was president of three wards at that time so he couldn't chair except in his wards but he could go to any meeting. He offered his opinions and when he was asked for them, he gave them. The club members appreciated having him and often asked for his advice. He began to be called "Mr. Democrat" around the Reading area and he truly was.

These clubs belonged to each district in the county whose members were the most seasoned Democrats. LeRoy could and did talk in all of the clubs and he became well known among them. He knew all the club members and knew all the county ward's chairmen. He was able to answer any question that was asked of him, or knew where to get the answer. Everyone knew how deeply he cared for the party as well as for the constituents.

LeRoy had to engage speakers for dinner parties for all the party members. He successfully engaged Senator Biden twice. Little did he know that the senator would become the 46th president. Throughout his long career in politics, LeRoy had the opportunity to meet several famous politicians, and he shared those stories with me.

He was able to get President Clinton to speak for the Democratic National Chairman's meeting. LeRoy had to have a special ticket to get into the lecture. Different ticket colors determined where you sat. He felt good because he thought he had a great seat. Suddenly, two men came up to him and asked if he was LeRoy Gensemer. They looked so official and LeRoy could not imagine what the problem was. They were Bill Clinton's bodyguards and they told him that Bill wanted him to sit closer to him. They escorted him to a different seat and he was four seats in front of the president. The president recognized him because he had set up and managed Clinton's headquarters in

Reading when the president was running for office. Of all the people he has met, he was most impressed with President Clinton. He felt that Bill Clinton was the most genuine man of them all. He talked to LeRoy in a down-to-earth manner and was downright friendly. He took the time to talk to each man who shook his hand. LeRoy must have been totally impressed because his opinion of the other 'notables' was that they were just there. Clinton was the exception. He was also exceptionally good looking and so much a people's guy.

LeRoy was invited to go to President Clinton's inaugural address. He was placed in the 20th row and sat next to a rather good-looking man but they had no conversation which was very unlike LeRoy. When the ceremony was over, a friend asked him if he knew who he had sat next to. LeRoy had no idea who he was. It turned out to be Will Smith, the famous actor, producer, and rapper. LeRoy did not keep up with famous people unless they were in his sphere of activity. He had little time for television or radio.

When John Kerry ran for president in 2004, he called the headquarters to ask if he could come up to Reading and wanted a short list of people to talk to for a short period of time. LeRoy was picked among the 20 who got to talk to him. Although LeRoy enjoyed meeting people with reputations such as Mr. Kerry, he was not in awe of them just because they were newsworthy. He had to feel good about them. He wasn't impressed with status. It was important what kind of person are you. He told very few people about these meetings, including me sometimes.

When President Kennedy ran for the presidency, he sent the Berks County Democratic Party $1,000, which no other candidate had ever done. The party was impressed.

President Lyndon Johnson spoke in Chicago for a Retail Clerks Union meeting which LeRoy was attending. LeRoy got to shake his hand and is proud of having shook hands with two presidents.

This union was another field where LeRoy was active. He seems to have been ubiquitous in his energy level and interests.

He often went to Harrisburg for parties organized for winning congressional candidates in the Democratic districts in the counties close to Harrisburg. LeRoy took responsibility for getting the beer and soda to the party room. On one occasion he could not find the wheeler to put the beverages on to get them to the proper room. He asked someone if they could tell him where to get one. The man asked him which party he belonged to and when LeRoy said he was a Democrat, the man told him where to get one. Another time when he was in Harrisburg for a meeting, a woman asked for directions to the room and when the person asked her which party she belonged to and she said Democrat, he told her to find the room herself. He found this to be typical of politicians.

Herbert Humphrey came to speak to the Democrats of Berks county. Anyone who wanted to talk to him had to pay $25. Many people bought time and the party made a nice sum of money. LeRoy paid and basically Hubert Humphrey took questions and answered them but gave no speech.

When Ed Rendell was running for governor of Pennsylvania, LeRoy was asked by a man if he knew him. LeRoy told him that he had held a meeting to promote Rendell and had been to his house and rode the campaign trail with him. Then he asked LeRoy if he knew Rendell's children. LeRoy told him no. The man said, "How can you campaign for a man you don't know." LeRoy responded, "I don't know God but I can stand here and talk about him." I was impressed with that response. I met Rendell one time and told him I was LeRoy's sister. His comment to me was, "You have a beautiful suit on." Period.

During one of these campaigns, an opposing candidate came to see LeRoy and his statement to LeRoy was, "I will win because my wife is prettier than your wife." LeRoy thought that to be such a ridiculous thing to say, but LeRoy won. The opponent was a lawyer which made the statement seem even more off the wall.

At different times, two council members asked LeRoy to endorse their candidacy, but he refused. He was unfamiliar with the councilmen's friends and he wanted to avoid supporting the wrong candidate. He also wanted to stay out of trouble with his Democratic friends so he remained neutral with all candidates throughout his political career.

A state representative from the 127th district called him a couple times to speak for him. LeRoy gladly accepted. He enjoyed speaking immensely and did it anytime someone asked him to, which was often. There's that positive attention again.

In 1999 LeRoy got deathly ill and was admitted to the hospital. The doctor told him there are 72 versions of the flu virus and he got the worst one. He was unable to walk or do anything for himself. The nurses were carrying him in a basket as he had lost so much weight. He would never ask me to come to see him, but I went often. On one of my visits we both cried and hugged because we thought this was going to be the end for him. He couldn't stop telling me he knew I would be there and he wanted so much to see me. It was one of his worst days. He spent some time in the ICU in a near death condition. He was such a sick man. He was in the hospital for 96 days plus 28 in rehab. I visited regularly but Sam never came, which was a huge disappointment to him. He had so many Democratic visitors and he was pleasantly surprised when Republicans came. While he was in the ICU a nurse told him he probably would never walk again. This was a terrible thing to say to him and he decided at that point to give up and not eat or take medications. He was not going to be a burden to his children. He looked toward the nurse's station and saw two men standing there. He knew they were evil and he said, "Lord, why did you send those evil men to bring me to you." He wanted to die. His lovely daughter-in-law came to see him and rubbed his shoulder, which to him was a huge amount of nurturing and he said it felt like heaven. Then she started to talk to him about the Lord. This gave him the impetus to live. He feels she saved his life. Wray had her own deprivation issues and was unable to do much nurturing, although I think she deeply loved him. While he was still sick but recovering, a county commissioner came to see him and asked him to get patients to register to vote. How crass! When he got home, LeRoy felt he had to go read the minutes for all the meetings he had missed. He discovered he was to be honored at the next meeting. When the member of the party was found out as the one who blew the surprise, he was severely chastised. LeRoy was shocked to think they would do this for him. It was hard for him to accept that he was honorable and important enough for the party to plan a big bash just for him. When there is no one to love you as a child, it is hard to believe that anything you do is noteworthy or that anyone would notice it or care. I can attest to those feelings.

The party decided to set up an annual award to be called the Democratic Achievement Award in 1995. Th first recipient was LeRoy and he was so touched. Until recently, he also had the distinction of holding more elected offices than anyone in Berks County had ever held. Now that record has been broken.

One night a man came to his house to ask for his support for a judgeship. He was cursing and using the f- word repeatedly. LeRoy is absolutely opposed to swearing, let alone to use that word, so he said to the candidate, "We don't swear in this house so get the hell out." The man left. LeRoy called a friend of his who was a Pennsylvania representative and supported this candidate. At his request, the representative withdrew his support. That candidate lost his bid for a judgeship.

The county commissioners did a charter study to decide whether it was feasible to eliminate 5 county offices. One was the jury commissioner and LeRoy held that position. He felt it was a vital position. The commissioners found out that there was a big farmer's convention convened at that time and figured that if they were to address the 1,200 or 1,300 farmers about this issue, it would be approved as a ballot measure on election day. The Democrats who wanted to eliminate the offices hired a lawyer to represent them and paid them $100 each, with the hope they could convince the farmers to vote with them. Their lawyer was to be the speaker for the commissioners. When the commissioners' lawyer got up to speak, someone in the back of the room yelled," You sound like a lawyer. Why don't you let LeRoy speak?" The lawyer turned the meeting over to LeRoy and he started out by saying, "I am here tonight to save your jobs and mine," After he spoke, he asked if anyone wanted to talk about the opposition's side. Someone said, "No. We trust you LeRoy" and there was no opposition. When it was on the ballot at the polls it failed. LeRoy made a habit of winning!

A county commissioner asked him to run for a state representative office. LeRoy told him that he thought he would be in over his head if he accepted. He reassured LeRoy that a secretary would do all the work. LeRoy felt that if he was unable to do the work himself, he couldn't accept the offer and he passed it up.

Abe Minker called LeRoy and asked him to grab a cab and go door to door to campaign for his choice for district attorney which LeRoy did because he felt Abe had been so good to him. That candidate won. A win again! Just as Abe appreciated his honesty, so did the public. They relied heavily on him for his opinions and feedback. He was so dedicated that if we were visiting him and the phone rang, if it was a political call, he would take it. Anyone else he would say he would call back. It is true that some politicians are caring people!

One night a county commissioner called LeRoy to say goodbye because he was tired of living and wanted to end it all. LeRoy called the police department and they sent people out to his house and saved him. The next day, the commissioner called

LeRoy and said, "You son of a bitch. You called the police." He wouldn't talk to LeRoy after that for a prolonged period of time but they later became friends and he thanked LeRoy for saving his life.

A Pennsylvania representative had passed away and LeRoy had worked very closely with him and knew him well, so of course, he went to the funeral. A man came up to LeRoy and started to talk to him. LeRoy said, "This is the biggest funeral I have ever seen. I'll never see another one bigger." The man said, "Yes, there will be a bigger one and that will be yours."

The Democratic Party put on a huge party for LeRoy because after 50 years he had decided it was time for him to retire. They gave him a proclamation which spelled out all he had accomplished in his lifetime in and out of politics. He treasures the memories of the party and the proclamation. Someone said to him at the party, "They will never find a sucker like you to do all the work you did." I believe it is true, as the party is not as active but LeRoy true to form, takes no credit for that. Some of his attributes that were good for the party were the same ones that allowed him to work with the Minkers: he never talked outside of the party, he was honest, he was willing to do any task, he was dependable, and he enjoyed the work and the camaraderie. He followed through on everything he said he would do. LeRoy and I talk about the fact that when we were at Bethany, you never told anyone that you would do something for them and then not follow through. We are both amazed that people do this all the time. We still feel that if you say you will, then you are bound by that. I know his grown-up children will be shocked to learn all he has done and it is all true. He did so many things he wouldn't talk about at the time but he still likes to "bull crap" as he calls it. Now talking is a habit. He told me that I know more about him than anyone and I believe it. We have always shared most of our problems and all the good things that happened to us over the years.

CHAPTER 9: CHARITIES

LEROY FORMED A BOND WITH BETHANY that has never been broken. He understood that when Bethany discharged him, they were trying to give him an opportunity to develop skills that would last him a lifetime so he had no hard feelings about his departure, but neither could he separate from "his home." After leaving he went back almost every weekend either to see Wray or to play sports, as he loved playing softball, volleyball, quoits and any other sports he could find people to play with. It was okay with Bethany for alumni to play because they had all the equipment, and the fields were not used on weekends. It was verboten to visit on the girl's side of the campus. If he was into the sports, they allowed this but not visiting girls.

When he came to see Wray, he never stopped to visit with me but somehow, I knew he loved me and I knew he felt the same. I wonder if at some level he felt responsible for me in our house of origin. That is the best we can figure out since we never had a relationship like this one with any of our other siblings. He is so family-minded he stayed in touch with all the siblings because they were all in Reading except me. He even planned some of their funerals.

Bethany wanted to form an alumni association since many former children were spending time there. It wasn't only LeRoy. LeRoy eventually became president of the association and remained so for 29 years. When he got into office, there were no rules governing process or tasks. LeRoy set up the by-laws and created offices with term limits. These by-laws were voted on and accepted, and the association now had purpose and meaning. Some of what they did was hold bake sales, and auctions. All members were alumni or relatives, such as spouses who wanted to support their partners. Siblings got involved also. At first, LeRoy supplied lunch for everyone. Eventually he asked the superintendent to feed the group, which he did if LeRoy set aside time to speak to the kids about his experiences at Bethany or how to succeed after Bethany. The deal was struck. The first time LeRoy wanted to run, he ran for the vice presidency. One member who was opposed to candidate running for president was upset that he was the only candidate. He began raising hell and put LeRoy's name in the mix. A vote was held and LeRoy won. A winner again!

They oversaw some big projects. Typically, the superintendent would tell the association a Bethany wish, LeRoy would propose it to the group, and they would vote on it. Some of the things they approved were the planting of 20 trees with plaques made in memory of deceased members of the association. They paid $650 to redo the tennis courts and $650 to build a badminton court, which LeRoy approved of wholeheartedly because he loved the sport and used their court often. They bought a grill to be used by the swimming pool which was built after our time. One member had business cards made for the group which they sold and made a profit of $200.

LeRoy planned two retreats and the superintendent allowed them to sleep over for free if they supplied their own food. These retreats were to reminisce about their days at Bethany with no business. They visited all the old haunts they remembered in the woods and the buildings where they lived, and played sports. Most of the members attended.

Anniversary Day was a huge affair for raising money for Bethany. The alumni had a spot under a huge tent put up for the occasion where they sold items such as used furniture or clothing, cakes, and candy. One member bought oodles of candy out of his own pocket and saw that the profits went to Bethany. LeRoy did a lot of the planning and setting up. As president he felt responsible for making it a success each year and it routinely was.

The superintendent asked LeRoy to suggest a volunteer for the Bethany Board of Managers. LeRoy suggested a woman who was active in the association. LeRoy's choice was turned down and because I was a social worker, I was chosen and served 10 years. LeRoy and the association were very upset about their choice, and he let me know they were, but it had no effect on our relationship.

The association developed an alumni award which was to be given to the alumni who contributed the most time or money to Bethany that year. LeRoy was awarded one, which he certainly earned. Years later I received one as well, but I felt someone else should have gotten it because I was not involved in any activity at Bethany. I had not been back even for a visit since I graduated from high school and I was then in my fifties.

Members began to die or to become ill and LeRoy saw that the membership was swiftly disintegrating. The younger Bethany graduates were not attached as some of our generation had been so they never made any effort to join, even though LeRoy gave them a pep talk before they departed. He told the superintendent that he decided to retire. The superintendent was furious, as we knew he would be. I had resigned after ten years, feeling that my contributions were underutilized and that I was being used as a token alumnus. To have an alumnus on the board looked good to the agencies who kept Bethany operating. The superintendent's comment was, "First your sister resigned from the board and now you." He understood that the association would fall apart once LeRoy retired and that he would lose a source of income. That was exactly what happened. LeRoy's retirement gift was his gavel and $600. He had paid Bethany back 100%. His only regret was that he could not get Wray involved. She was not opposed to LeRoy being involved but she was now into being home and did not go out much.

In addition to his work at Bethany, LeRoy volunteered for several other organizations over the years, as well as for his church.

Redner's Markets made a deal with LeRoy about 25 years ago. The receipt someone receives when they pay with the store's reward card is recorded and LeRoy gets a copy. He calculates 1% of all the money spent and turns the receipts back to the store. They check LeRoy's math and give these proceeds to LeRoy's church. The money adds up to about $400 a year. He is now 92 and still collects them.

He was appointed by the Berks County Court to be a member of the Youth Aid Program. This program was started because the courts were swamped with cases. His job was to talk to youth who had committed minor crimes, such as shoplifting, and to ascertain what their punishment should be. The hope was that these kids would not have second offenses. He did this for 8 years for Berks County kids.

LeRoy was also a volunteer for two senior programs for church members who were over 50. He was a member of one of the churches, which is how he got involved. The people paid $1 per month to the church for programming. One of these groups appointed LeRoy as their president. He called bingo for the players in both groups on a weekly basis and the person who won received prizes, such as apartment necessities like canned goods or paper products.

He planned trips for them to local places and the church members who went paid for the trip. It raised money for other programming he planned. He organized picnics and they often played bingo after they ate. They paid to play and the winner for the day received whatever was in the pot. Some days as I write, I get tired just thinking about LeRoy's boundless energy. My family thinks I have a lot too. I think being busy kept him from ever having to deal with his deprivation, and that is a good thing.

LeRoy called bingo until a problem developed. The women who sat in the front row started to vie for his attention. They bought him gifts and food. This angered the rest of the group. When romantic implications developed, he left. He was known throughout the Reading area as the best bingo caller, and called at clubs, churches, and social events.

For Christmas they had about 85 people at one senior group party and 100 at the other. All attendees paid $5 for this affair. One group met at a hotel and the other in a church for a meal and candy. Then there was entertainment. Everyone looked forward to what was probably their only seasonal party. LeRoy also went to Wernersville State Hospital for a few Christmases and sang carols, read the bible, and socialized.

He engaged speakers or other entertainment every month and was totally responsible for organizing all of the programming. After 6 or 7 years of working with these groups, the clubs closed. One because the church could no longer give them enough parking spaces and the other for a lack of attendance.

LeRoy was also a volunteer Sunday school teacher for 5th and 6th graders and later he taught seniors. This was a job he did for years and years. Twice he took one of his classes to a picnic and the pastor was nervous because of the problems that could occur if someone got hurt. He warned LeRoy he would be responsible. LeRoy took the chance and there were no incidents. He planned sleepovers in the church with both boys and girls but he had a woman with the girls to avoid problems for himself. He took this on for 12 years and resigned because he developed a new interest. One can never say he let grass grow under his feet. What amazes me was how he juggled so many things simultaneously.

He always participated in sports at the same time he was pursuing his many other interests.

He wanted to learn more about the policeman's and fireman's job responsibilities so he took their training courses and climbed the ladders, rode with the police at night, met their dogs and completed the tests. When he had completed these courses he was given a plaque. He never signed up to work but he was happy about the plaque and the enjoyment he got from the training. He was 83 at that time.

CHAPTER 10: SPORTS

BETHANY NEEDED THE BOYS ON THE FARM which meant there was no time for sports. When they did have free time they formed a softball team. One day a matron suggested to LeRoy that he pitch lefthanded. He still doesn't know why the matron made this comment, but LeRoy obeyed and learned to pitch with either hand. They also played quoits and horseshoes and LeRoy always did well. He competed with himself and improved his skills with no coach. Sports were always part of the itinerary each time he went to Bethany. Their equipment was the drawing card and he couldn't afford to pay anywhere else.

After LeRoy left Bethany, he heard about roller skating in Sinking Springs. He was single and this was a new sport for him, but he took to it immediately. He bought a cheap secondhand pair of skates for $25 and started skating. No one taught him what to do, he just watched good skaters and copied them. Soon he was one of the best at the rink. He knew all the dances and skated with the best of the female skaters. He saw Wray on weekends and dated many of the skaters during the week. One of the skaters was smitten with him. On one of their dances together she said to him, "Why don't you ask me out". He said, "You have dated all these skaters, why me?" She responded, "Ask me out." He did and they dated for 3 months, but never on weekends because that was Wray's time. She ended the relationship to move to New York to become a model. She sent LeRoy a picture of herself posing in a bathing suit, which he kept until Wray found it and discarded it.

Institutionalized and Happy

He became such a proficient skater that he needed to buy good skates. He told Wray the new skates would cost $125, but actually bought a pair for $225. He deserved them because he was so dedicated to the sport. He had to save to buy these and that was tough, but he was determined. At that time he earned $19 per week! He went to parties each night after skating, which were held at a different skater's house. It was a tight group. I watched him one night and could not believe my eyes. He was so graceful and such a professional - he was absolutely the best dancer in the rink. He was so involved in his skating I doubt that he ever saw me. At that time I had no idea he had a talent for sports or that he loved competition, as I was fresh out of Bethany and never knew of his activities. I was flabbergasted by his skills. Eventually, he had to give it up after he started a family. He could no longer afford it and I felt as bad about that as he did. He was a beautiful skater.

LeRoy's Sunday ritual was to ride bikes with his kids to nearby towns, such as Womelsdorf, Boyertown, and Kutztown. Sometimes his daughter-in-law would ride along with them. On his last ride, Carol and he went alone. He loved cycling for years.

LeRoy became a big fan of badminton after first playing a version of the game with a tennis ball on a volleyball court in 1982. Once he saw that he was good at it, he routinely went to local high schools to play and practice. He felt he was good enough to compete in the county Olympic senior competition for 55 and older. He not only played badminton but quoits, horseshoes, stationary bikes, and bowling. He went to colleges too, including Shippensburg. The competitors paid $50 for room, board, and evening entertainment. Bocce Ball with snacks and drinks was available all day and evening. No alcohol was served but LeRoy never drank those types of drinks in his whole life. When I make fruitcake I add brandy and rum - LeRoy won't eat it even though he loves it! He was quite successful at these games. He competed in Berks, Chester, and Lebanon counties after a law was passed to allow competitors to play outside of their county. He won most of his games which was the impetus for him to go to the state level senior Olympics.

He played the same sports at the state Olympic level. There the competition was stronger. The game he enjoyed most was badminton. To no one's surprise he also won most of those competitions. He was having a respiratory problem. I suggested he go to an acupuncturist who had helped me over the years. He had been a pathologist and then a medical doctor. The doctor thought he could not treat certain patients as he wanted to, and felt he could do more for them as an acupuncturist. He felt there were few good acupuncturists because it was a demanding course of studying if you did it right. He frowned on the skills of most acupuncturists because most were inadequately trained. During the Second World War many people were trained in China so the government could put one in every region of the country. He studied for years while the Chinese system took only a few months. He eventually became the top acupuncturist in the area and headed their organization. LeRoy was thrilled he was able to make the respiratory problem better in just a few visits, as he had been a very heavy smoker at 3 packs of cigarettes per day. For years, I had repeatedly asked him to stop and eventually (years later) he did. Three of our siblings died from smoking-related disorders and I wanted him around for many years. He quit cold turkey in 1978 because he was coughing so much it interfered with his political speeches.

Later, right before a game, he experienced some shoulder pain and tried the same acupuncturist. He treated LeRoy, and gave him two needles to place in his ears before the game. He did as was instructed and won that badminton match. When the game was won he felt extremely tired and Wray told him the needles had fallen out. He was needled (no pun intended) by the other players for wearing them but was determined to do as he was told and credits those needles for winning.

An alumna from Bethany asked LeRoy to become a partner at the games for doubles badminton. He played with her several times, but after losing a few times he never partnered with her again. It went against the grain for him to lose. Now he felt ready to tackle the nationals. Though he was unable to win any medals at that level, the camaraderie and competition excited him.

One time LeRoy was to compete with a man who was Pennsylvania State Olympic Champion in badminton. After the games, he challenged LeRoy to another game saying that LeRoy wouldn't even get two points from him. LeRoy took him up on it and, although he lost, he did gain the two points. He played at these three levels of Olympics for 31 years and loved every minute he played. He was in his backyard one day and fell on a rake and was severely injured. That ended his career with competition with deep regret.

Before the accident, he was also able to play softball on the team at his church, which competed with other churches in the area. Each 4th of July they had a contest to see who could throw a ball the farthest and LeRoy won that contest until he was 86. It boggles my mind to think of what he won without any formal training. He had to be a gifted athlete. He won 65 Pennsylvania State Olympic medals over his lifetime and proudly displayed them in his basement, but was particular about who he showed them to. He was not the type to brag and knew that some visitors might interpret this display as such. He had a special case for the medals and was almost prouder of the metals than of what he had done to earn them. Of all the sports he had played badminton was his best, and the record he was most proud of.

He now plays two games in his retirement home. One is Corn Hole, where you throw a bean bag through a hole. He can still win this game at 92. He will never get over winning. That gets him the positive attention he has always craved. I believe that all of the challenges he's faced in his life played into this desire, and he planned it right.

CHAPTER 11:
BUSINESS CARDS

IN 1986, LEROY WENT TO VISIT A LAWYER FRIEND OF HIS who had a daughter 10 years of age. He commenced to talk to her about her hobby of collecting business cards. She showed him the collection she had amassed. She was extremely proud of her cards and she suggested to LeRoy that he should start collecting them too. Because LeRoy thought it was an odd thing to do, he decided to do it. Before long he was into this new hobby bigtime, as he always was in whatever he did.

He started asking everyone he met and anyone he knew to give him their business card. He was still in the political world at this time so he collected from every politician he knew, which was a lot of people. He went into offices in Harrisburg, the Pennsylvania state capital, where he knew lots of people and he was on his way to becoming one of the biggest collectors of business cards in the world. Maybe even the biggest.

Anytime he went to restaurants or stores he looked for their card and took a few because he now was trading them all over the country. There were times when he and Wray traveled around the local stores or in neighboring towns to pick up any card they could find. They went into every retail store and office. One time, LeRoy was pulled over by a state policeman for speeding on a street near Philadelphia. After the policeman was through issuing LeRoy a $90 ticket, LeRoy asked him for a business card. The policeman was confused and LeRoy never told him why he wanted it. I guess the policeman was worried LeRoy was going to make trouble for him but he eventually gave his card to him. LeRoy always imagined him going home and telling his wife about this weird request and saying it was some nut!

By this time, I was traveling overseas to many countries. In every country I visited I stopped in city halls to collect their business cards. What wonderful experiences I had! Sometimes I got a city tour, a cake, gossip about the royal family of England, flags, and all kinds of political buttons. Sometimes I got a business card from every person in the building. When I went to Malta one summer all of the politicians were on summer break. The man in charge of the building asked me to leave my address and said he would send me the congresses' cards. Sure enough, I later got at least 30 cards in the mail. This happened more than once so I began to leave LeRoy's card for them, so they could mail their cards directly to him. If my husband was on the trip with me, he would get embarrassed and wait outside, but he eventually got over that. He missed seeing so many beautiful buildings. Sometimes he did go in with me and he remembers how beautiful the rooms were as we toured the Cardiff City Hall. The information we learned about these buildings was educational and interesting, especially when our guide proceeded to tell us some royal gossip. She had dated one of the family and danced in the beautiful ballroom in that City Hall. My husband was glad he visited and eventually began to pick up cards himself. I always started out by telling these people that I had a crazy request to make. Some people thought it was weird, but others thought it was neat. Either way they gave up their cards!

LeRoy wrote letters to about 60 celebrities and got many of their cards. One of the first people to respond was Frank Sinatra. Sinatra was his favorite singer so that was a gold mine for him. He plays Frank Sinatra music almost every day and has for years. LeRoy came to Philadelphia a few times for Frank's concerts.

He also wrote to Dave Letterman and on his nightly show one night he told his audience that he got a letter from a LeRoy Gensemer from Reading, Pennsylvania who asked him for a business card. He sent one but thought it was a weird request. LeRoy heard about it later and someone gave him a tape of the show. Unfortunately, it got lost in his latest move. I am disappointed he never told me so I have not heard it.

LeRoy wrote to presidents of the United States for their cards and usually got them. He never got one from Barack Obama but he did get a response in letter from him. He requested cards from Donald Trump but got no response. I had previously tried to get Trump's card when he owned the big casino in Atlantic City but to no avail.

For years LeRoy found cards in his mailbox. No one ever left any names so he could never thank them. He was thrilled to get them however.

He decided to become the biggest collector of Century 21 cards. Pretty soon I was bringing them to him also. One time I was in Palm Springs and saw the Century 21 office. We stopped the car and went into the store. I proceeded to say why I came and a man spoke up and told me that Century 21 had yearly meetings in Florida, and when they held the next one he would call me and have all the members pass their cards to the aisle. It turns out that he was the owner of Century 21! Unfortunately, this plan never came to fruition, but LeRoy still amassed 38,000 of their cards. He got most of them by writing to every Century 21 office he could find in the phone book. I went into one Century 21 office and asked for their cards. I got zippo because they suspected I wanted them for some nefarious reason. It shocked me. What could I do with them except give them to a collector? I had the same experience in a local city hall.

Mary Kay was his next big interest and he collected over 8,000 of those. A man in California was giving up collecting and sent

LeRoy all of his cards. Many belonged to these two businesses and that got him started.

The mother of the 10-year-old girl who got LeRoy into this hobby also began to collect cards. She was originally from Tennessee and went down for a visit with her family. She visited a flea market and discovered a card that belonged to a club called Card Talk. She and LeRoy contacted the club and decided to join. They put out a brochure every month which LeRoy still subscribes to. He learned where events were occurring and decided to execute plans of his own. One time he made plans with the club to set up tables and manage a meeting for the purpose of trading cards in Fort Washington, Pennsylvania. He went to the podium, gave his name, and talked. A man from New Jersey came to LeRoy and asked if he was the man from Reading. LeRoy said he was, and from then on when he came to LeRoy's area, he would stay at LeRoy's house and they traded cards.

A man from Iowa traveled all over the world to get cards. LeRoy traded with him and decided that since he was coming monthly, he would invite the club to his house every 1st Saturday in August and have the members trade cards. LeRoy hosted a luncheon with donuts and coffee in the morning, but supper was on them. He did this for 29 years. He got about 20 or 10 attendees toward the end but decided to quit holding the event because interest was waning.

LeRoy also set up a card trading event in Tennessee. He and Wray went down for two days. LeRoy paid for all the pizzas and hoagies for lunch. He hoped to have 100 people but had 75. By the time he was ready to drive home his trunk was fully loaded with the cards he had traded and he got a flat tire. He dreaded having to empty his trunk to get to his spare. Luckily, a man stopped by and told him he would do it for him. He emptied the whole trunk, got the tire, changed it, and put everything back in the trunk. LeRoy asked him what the charge would be. He answered, "Nothing. I have more money than you." The man did not have a business card. LeRoy never failed to ask!

He was in Reading at the courthouse one winter day and a man needed jump cables. He asked LeRoy if he had them and LeRoy told him that if he wanted to borrow them, it would cost him. You guessed it! He wanted 5 business cards. He told the man he would have to pay up or there would be no jump. He turned out to be a banker. He paid up and LeRoy jumped his battery.

The time came for LeRoy to move to a retirement home and he decided to leave the business. At this time he had 2,590,200 cards. He put an ad in the Card Talk brochure and through word of mouth sold all he was able to and the rest went into a dumpster. He was proud of the fact that he had received a plaque from "Ripley's Believe It or Not" for having the biggest collection without duplicates. He was told by a member in England that LeRoy had the world's biggest collection. That was an unofficial remark and it never was proven, but LeRoy believes it is probably true. He was able to walk away with $4,000 for his sold cards. He is still collecting for one friend and talks to a few collectors. He is not sorry he gave it up as he is keeping busy at the retirement home with games and Redner's Market.

CHAPTER 12:
HIS MARRIAGE AND FAMILY

I sat on these steps and said, "I think I am going to marry Wray Miller."

BACK AT BETHANY, WHEN LEROY WAS 15, his job was to take care of the trash in the Speese building, which overlooked the girl's ironing room in Santee. There were about 10 girls ironing men's shirts with irons from the stove. The irons were used until they cooled off and then they went back on the stove to reheat. If you were lucky there was another hot one to use to finish your shirt. Often there wasn't another one hot enough to use immediately so we stood around waiting for them to heat, and then your shirt dried out. It was a frustrating job. Wray was ironing at that time and LeRoy looked down and told himself, "That is the most beautiful girl I have ever seen and someday I will marry her." He was satisfied with just a look until he discovered she was roller skating around the Administration building every day. Before anyone ever heard of a skateboard, LeRoy built one so he could skate with her. That was the start of their relationship.

On Sundays we were off the hook for work because the Bible said you rest on the 7th day. Wray and a friend would walk off campus after church to a store we called the "One Mile Sign" because it was a mile from Bethany. It sold candy, soda, and other snack foods. They carried the group's favorite orange soda, which they drank every Sunday they could afford it. LeRoy would arrange to meet them. This became a weekly walk, and I cannot figure out how they avoided getting caught. Most of us were caught all the time. You had to pass the farm and houses along the walk so people were available to rat on you all along the way. A punishment always came along with ignoring the rules. One lovely Sunday the three of them did their usual Sunday trip. LeRoy and Wray never let on to each other that they knew they were in love. LeRoy, who was 15 at this time, was told that if he kissed a girl on the lips, she would become pregnant. He believed it, as I bet their friend did also. They had been holding hands but never had they kissed. That Sunday LeRoy saw a log near the road and took Wray to it where they shared their first kiss. The friend must have believed Wray got pregnant and reported her. She must have been very worried because we rarely ratted on each other. Only if the situation was larger than we felt we could manage did we feel we needed an intervention from the superintendent. That night at chapel LeRoy had to sit alone and the sermon was about his "sin" and bad behavior. Too often any bad behavior from someone was aired at chapel services. The sermons were planned around that behavior. There was no tolerance for romance or sexual acting out. Any transgressions dealing with sex were so bad that you had to be expelled from Bethany.

When LeRoy was no longer at Bethany he hitchhiked back every weekend to visit Wray. He was not supposed to go to the girl's side of campus but he would show up at Wray's cottage, which was next to the superintendent's cottage, and ask one of the girls to find her for him. They visited on or off campus. Somehow this must have been sanctioned by the superintendent because they were never caught. I checked with LeRoy to be sure about this because it would have been a great big serious offense to be caught dating on campus.

On one occasion, LeRoy hitchhiked with Wray to Himmelreich's Grove. It was a glorious summer day and the two lovers were out for a good time. They spent the day at the grove and after dark decided to take a walk in the woods. The walk led to their having their first sexual encounter. They were so happy that they forgot about getting Wray home in time. Bethany was out of its mind. You were in trouble if you missed a meal or bedtime. Wray had missed two meals and bedtime. She knew she was in big trouble. Early Monday morning, before she could talk to the other girls, she was told to go to the infirmary where she was checked to see if she had lost her virginity. They ascertained that she had, and she was taken to Ringtown that same day (in the coal regions of Pennsylvania) to live with her sister. She was permanently gone from Bethany.

LeRoy hitchhiked every weekend to see her. After a while Wray wanted to be closer to him so she moved to Reading where she got a job as a live-in maid with a doctor and his family. When she was free she would see him. On weekends they hitchhiked to Easton to see a movie or just to look around. They were having sex on these visits and decided that if he impregnated her they would get married. In those days, that was almost an automatic solution. In fact, if someone was talking about a friend, it was not uncommon to say, "Did you know they *had* to get married" meaning it in a derogatory way. They both agreed to this plan. She did become pregnant and they got married in their church with no one present. They went to Philadelphia for their honeymoon and saw a movie. He never proposed but they were so in love, they just got married. LeRoy was 20 and Wray was 18. I always felt it was almost a robotic relationship, they just got married. Whatever happened just happened, and you figured out as they happened what to do about it. Shades of Bethany training.

One time they were hitchhiking back from Easton where they had gone to a movie. Wray was pregnant first her first child, Bruce, and she had to go to the bathroom so LeRoy found a secluded place off the highway where she could relieve herself while LeRoy stood on guard for her. Suddenly a car appeared. A policeman got out, shined a flashlight on LeRoy, and asked him why he was there. LeRoy told him his wife was going to the bathroom and would he please turn the flashlight off. The policeman did just that. He asked them where they were headed and LeRoy said to Reading. The policeman told them to get in his car and he would give them a ride. He drove them to the local diner and asked if anyone there was going to Reading. A truck driver said he was, so the policeman arranged the trip and left. The trucker bought them a meal (benefiting from a freebie again!) and drove them to their home in Reading. In that time, you knew you were usually safe thumbing.

Their first apartment was small and costly for them. It was $18 a month. Wray was not working, and LeRoy was still working at Cassells. They could not afford to furnish it, so LeRoy brought to the apartment the paper they used at Cassells to wrap lunch meat and that became their rug. They had a bed and a chair and empty crates from the store which became their storage space. Wray's hospital bill for Bruce's delivery was $50, which they paid off in installments. The doctor who employed Wray was kind to them. He delivered all of her children for free and saw the children for their follow-up appointments. That sure was a good thing because they were poor. I never saw LeRoy unhappy during all of his poor days.

A few times they took Bruce with them as they continued to hitchhike. They went to neighboring towns to see movies or just to walk around and see if anything was going on. Poverty did not curtail their need to keep busy. They wouldn't allow anything to get under their feet. They never thought of moving away from Reading, nor did LeRoy think of changing jobs. He was just there, and he continued the Bethany way of life, which was do what you must, get it done, and do not question. Just keep moving and stay busy.

Two years later Wray was pregnant with her second child, so they needed more space. They had to move to a larger apartment which cost $24 a month. This one had a flat roof and one time later he saw his 3 years old son, Walter, walking on it alone and rescued him. Thank goodness or we might not have that great guy today.

Playgrounds were popular in those days and they were free. They sent their kids there every day to use the playground equipment such as swings and to utilize whatever the supervisors had planned for the day. It was a safe and comfortable place for kids. On Friday nights they could watch a movie and get a free chocolate milk. What a treat for kids coming from poor families.

One-night LeRoy had a meeting to go to so he sent Jay to the playground. A babysitter was out of the question because he couldn't afford one. He told Jay not to leave unless his dad came to pick him up. Everyone left but Jay who was crying because LeRoy ran late. A policeman came and asked Jay what he was doing there. Jay told him, "I have to stay until my dad comes." The policeman took him to the station and Jay was a wreck when his dad picked him up. This mortified LeRoy as he was not the type of dad who was usually late. He cared so much about being a good dad - like the one he missed out on.

When they had four children LeRoy had to go to the hospital to have his appendix taken out. Sam went with him and as LeRoy was wheeled into the operating room, Sam said to him, "Die, son of a bitch, die." I was stunned when he told me because it sounded so horrible. LeRoy explained that that was said often at Bethany and it was meant as good luck. When Sam had his appendix taken out later LeRoy said the same thing to him. Odd because LeRoy has always hated swearing, as did Sam.

The family had a wagon and just like their father the children were clever about making money. They took their wagon, picked up old newspapers and telephone books, and brought them to a lumber yard where they got a nickel a piece for them. Walter, the entrepreneur, had some other kids pick them up for him and he paid them one cent each. When Walter took them to the lumber yard he still made four cents for himself. They were always allowed to keep money they earned, even though their parents could have used it.

Each Sunday the family went to church. Wray usually walked them there because LeRoy was working, but if she slept late LeRoy would arrange to take them. They often picnicked at a nearby dam and Sunday was a good day for that.

Donna was their 5th child and Dean followed 4 years later. Donna was delighted because she thought the baby was hers. Her parents had to tell her it was their child. She was so upset and cried quite hard, but she never ceased being a little mother to him.

A few times Bruce and Walter hitchhiked with their dad to Philadelphia to see professional baseball at Shibe Park. LeRoy thought all boys should see professionals' play. He has no memory of how he sneaked into the park, but he knows he did because he could not afford to pay. He was ecstatic to think he could see his boys enjoy professional baseball. They hitchhiked home.

Christmas was a big day for the family. LeRoy always bought a tree but only put it up after the kids went to bed on Christmas Eve - just like Bethany did for us. On Christmas morning, the kids had to go down the back steps, eat breakfast, and clean up before they got to see the tree or their presents. Bethany did that too. Later, they went to church. The church was and still is important to LeRoy. He still goes every Sunday.

For Christmas each child could write 5 things they wanted and their parents would spend $250 to get them what was on their list. LeRoy paid for the gifts on time, but it took him a year to pay them all off. By then it was time for Christmas again and he would repeat the process.

When Dean, the youngest, was only 8 years old he wrote for his five items: beer cans, beer cans, beer cans, beer cans, beer cans. LeRoy asked him what he meant, and he said it was a great way to make money. It turned out to be a tremendous gift. It was a big collectors' craze of that time. They turned his big idea into a business. LeRoy borrowed $450 to start the business and they became big fast. So big that LeRoy paid his debt off in 2 weeks. They soon became the third largest collector on the east coast and he had the biggest variety of cans. His garage was his place of business and in a short time the garage was overloaded. The way to sell them was to open them from the bottom and empty them leaving the top intact

They started buying empty cans from a brewery and paid $8 for a case of 24 cans. He charged $1 a can. He progressed into buying the cans from individuals and they did what they called "dumping." They went to landfills in the coal region, salvaged all of the beer cans, cleaned them, and sold them. One day when they had just finished dumping (and hadn't yet cleaned the cans), a man came along and asked if he could buy the cans. The value of the cans was undetermined, but they had 3 large bags. LeRoy and the man set the price at $400 and they were sold. Who knows what they might have gotten for them individually but LeRoy thinks it was a great deal.

A Bethany alum came to put LeRoy out of business and bought cases from Dean at $8 per case. Later, LeRoy put him out of business and bought the same cases back for $6 per case. Another dealer came to buy and bought $400 worth of cases. He later put this man out of business too.

No one in the family liked to drink beer so they would go to an alley to open the cans from the bottom and pour the beer down the drain. One day LeRoy saw a policeman sitting in his car in the alley. LeRoy thought he was going to get bawled out for not registering his business. He was nervous when the cop came over and said, "What are you doing?" LeRoy explained and the cop asked him if he could go home and bring back a pitcher so he could have some beer. LeRoy told him that would be fine with him and the policeman did come back with a pitcher. LeRoy did not charge him.

The whole family helped Dean, but the profits were his. He made $27,000 the first year with a profit of 50 to 60%.

When I traveled overseas, I would bring home as many cans as I could. I emptied them so I was not doing anything illegal. One man from Ohio came for quite a few cases which had not been emptied. LeRoy was worried he would get in trouble crossing state lines, but the man got home without incident.

One day Dean was not home, and a man came by and asked LeRoy if he wanted some Cloud 9 cans. LeRoy did not know what to do because Dean was the price setter. He took a chance and bought 12 for $1 a can and sold them for $2 a can. He was dreading Dean coming home and telling him how badly he had done but when he came home, he told him about the transaction. Dean only wanted to know if the man had more. It was one of the rare brands.

Institutionalized and Happy

In 1955, LeRoy was still working at Cassells and still struggling to support his family. He needed a house because his family now consisted of four boys and one girl. He borrowed and eventually paid back $600 for the down payment, but when he got to settlement he discovered he was $60 short. The realtor loaned him the $60 and it took LeRoy one year to repay him. They got the house and lived there for quite a few years. He walked 4 miles to work because he could not afford the price of the bus. Every penny was going to his family. He was so broke that one day he said to Wray, "We never planned any of our children so let us try for one more because we will be poor all the rest of our lives anyway." It never came to fruition. He loved those kids and was totally happy despite being broke.

When the kids were all in school, Wray got a night shift job at Luden's, known for their cough drops. She enjoyed the job, and it eased the financial situation somewhat. She got a pension when she retired and that was a big bonus. The kids have since told their dad that they were unaware of being poor.

When Bruce was 10 days old LeRoy joined a softball team called the BooBoos. Everyone started to call Bruce "BooBoo" and still do. I never liked that nickname so he was always Bruce to me. Bruce tells me that he doesn't mind BooBoo but when LeRoy talks about him to me, he calls him Bruce. For me it sounds like a child's name. He is now 72.

Bruce wanted to join the Boy Scouts and LeRoy became a scout master's assistant. They managed to get to one Valley Forge Jamboree which was a big deal in scouting. Eventually, Bruce lost interest so they both left that part of their lives behind them.

Dean wanted to be an Indian Guide. Each person involved had to take a name and LeRoy had the name Big Cloud and Dean was Little Cloud. Nine boys were involved. They had to have their fathers with them weekly or they could not join. They took turns hosting monthly meetings in each boy's house. This was supposed to be a one-year stint but it continued for 3 years. They arranged small trips like visiting City Hall or they told Indian stories and made crafts. One time they planted a tree at Albright College and the college provided a plaque designating it as their tree.

LeRoy played horseshoes at the county park and took some of the kids with him. He found out when the game was over that two of the kids were taking bets from other visitors that their dad's team would win. The kids made money.

During WWII LeRoy got a draft notice to serve. When he went to the draft board to report, they discussed his occupation and family situation. When he said he had six children, the recruiter told him, "Get rid of those kids and we will take you." LeRoy was unwilling to do that under any circumstances, so he never served. I know that was the right decision.

Soon the three oldest boys were ready to leave for the service. They all left at the same time. Walter went to California to learn how to repair helicopters. One day he was told he would be sent to Vietnam to be a gunner in a Huey. The officer who gave Walter this new assignment told Walter he was such a lucky guy because all the guys in the room wanted that job. LeRoy turned around to the group and asked how many of them wanted to do it. No one wanted it. LeRoy turned around to the officer and said "You are a bull shitter." Walter served two tours by choice as a gunner in a Huey. LeRoy was upset with himself because he swore but he had a hard time accepting the officer lying to his son.

Two of the boys spent time in Vietnam. Walter and Jay were there at the same time and Jay was able to make a surprise visit to visit Walter. Walter was sleeping in his bunk so Jay went to his bed and pulled at his brother's toes. What a surprise that was! The guys met a few times, and it was wonderful for them. All three guys came back safely but Walter still has problems related to his service, so he understands veterans' problems well. He works tirelessly for them and we both are so proud of his accomplishments. They all came back home when they returned from Vietnam. They left as they decided to marry, but still visited home often to spend time with their parents and their siblings.

By the time the kids were all out of the house, LeRoy had no need for all that space and the neighborhood was becoming unsafe. They moved to Exeter in a nice little house with some nice grounds. For the first time LeRoy realized that he and Wray no longer had anything in common. Their interests were not in sync and she liked being home much more than LeRoy did. Their interests at home were also different. Instead of looking at the marriage, LeRoy kept himself busy with the family and got involved with activities outside of his home. Through his interests he had become a social butterfly. He invited Wray to go wherever he went, but she stayed home. He felt he had outgrown her. Her world was too small for him. One time he told me he was going to get an apartment and leave her, but he never did it. He wanted to keep the family together. He rarely got angry at people but he said he could get very angry with his wife, and sometimes he wasn't the nicest person to be around. He paced when he was angry and when he couldn't take anymore, he cursed at her in spite of his hatred for cursing. I believe (and LeRoy believes) that she loved him until her death. Her last words to him were "I love you."

LeRoy wanted to stay in the house and continue operating his roofing business. He kept everything pertaining to that in his truck in the drive. One day an officer from the county came to his house to tell him that because he was in a residential area, he was unable to continue roofing from that site. LeRoy told him all the business was in his truck, but the officer said "no go" so the business was done.

Wray was to have a colonoscopy one day in 2012, but instead of going through the usual routine of cleaning out with fluids she went to the hospital with no preparation. The doctor did something she called a vacuum which made her so sick that she had to go to the hospital the next day. The hospital discovered what had happened and the doctor who performed the 'vacuum procedure' was fired. Wray was stuck with problems this doctor caused for the rest of her life. Her health went downhill from there. She developed kidney and heart problems and was sick on and off for the rest of her life. She required a walker, which ended a lot of their activities except short rides or going out to eat. She no longer cooked any meals and LeRoy never learned that skill. There were times when she was sick, but if one of her sons offered to take her to a flea market or a casino it seemed to perk her up. She was in and out of the hospital at least a dozen times and her problems became more than LeRoy could handle. She lived in 3 different facilities before they found a lovely one in a beautiful setting. Each time she ended up back in the hospital, which was the impetus for another move. LeRoy visited her at each place once a week. It affected her in such a way she would get angry at family members and not speak to them for prolonged periods. I made that list right up to her death. At 84 she died. Many politicians came to the funeral and it was a nice ceremony planned by her children. LeRoy and I walked away together, and he confessed that it was a relief for him, as he was always an upbeat person who could not relate to her unhappiness. She had been unhappy for years and thought it was all LeRoy's or one of the children's fault.

After Wray died LeRoy remained busy with his business cards, volunteer work, and politics so he was content to live alone for 4 years in his house. Bruce suggested that he should go to a retirement community. I kept telling him to make the decision to go when he was ready. At this time he had the rake accident and was hospitalized for a while. They cleaned out the house of anything LeRoy wanted out. He was happy as a clam at first. All his children were aces to him and still are. They played cards with him or did whatever they asked him to do. Often, they played a game called Dice with him, which he enjoyed. Donna brought him his food until she moved to another town to be near her son. He replaced Donna's home cooking with Meals on Wheels. He worked hard on his business cards and was busy enough to be contented. His children provided meals, rides to doctors, shopping, and whatever else he needed. They were even willing to drive him to see me and will continue to do so after the COVID-19 goes away. Of course, he tells me he will be here for lunch and I happily serve him.

Eventually LeRoy began to feel lonely and decided the time had come for him to give up the house. He wanted to keep it as an inheritance for his kids, but they convinced him they didn't need it so he willingly gave it up for a lovely retirement home in a beautiful setting, which of course his children found for him. He is still into sports and has a team for quoits and plays Corn Hole, the bean bag game. Now he says he wishes he had gone to Heritage Greens in Reading earlier. I remind him that we can only be where we are at the time and he had to make his own decision. Only after he went did he fully realize what a people person he is. My daughter Patricia always wondered if he was lonely in his house because ever since he was in the grocery business and politics, he was a big people person and that is how she knows him to be. He said he never realized how much he missed people. Now he is surrounded by them. After meals he loves to sit in the dining room and "bull crap." He is as happy as a clam.

LeRoy is in fair health, with some of his problems related to years of smoking and the rest related to his accident. He is 92 and happy, regardless of his health issues. When he tells me about his aches and pains, he always adds, "But I'll be all right, sis." We see little of each other because of COVID-19. I live outside of Philadelphia and he is in Reading. We talk almost every day, especially while I was interviewing him and questioning him for this book. One day I didn't need to ask any more questions and he congratulated me.

He is proud of these final two stories because they make him feel he left a mark in life. One day he went to Penn State with Alverney College's coach, who he met through politics. A man came up to the coach and asked him if he knew LeRoy Gensemer. To be known outside of his area was meaningful to him. Was that another medal? Another time he was on the turnpike and accidentally forgot to pay with his E-ZPass. He turned around and went to the window to explain and to pay his ticket. The lady at the counter said, "LeRoy Gensemer get out of here" and would not accept his money. Another medal. He feels certain he has left his mark in this world. I agree. That is the brother I love, LeRoy.

www.ingramcontent.com/pod-product-compliance
Lightning Source LLC
Chambersburg PA
CBHW061956070426
42450CB00011BA/3119